50 Raw Food Diet Recipes for Home

By: Kelly Johnson

Table of Contents

- Green Goddess Salad
- Zucchini Noodles with Pesto
- Raw Pad Thai
- Mango Salsa
- Coconut Curry Wraps
- Rainbow Veggie Rolls
- Cashew Cheese Stuffed Peppers
- Beet and Avocado Carpaccio
- Cucumber Gazpacho
- Cauliflower Tabouli
- Almond Butter Energy Balls
- Sprouted Quinoa Salad
- Raw Chocolate Avocado Mousse
- Carrot Ginger Soup
- Raw Falafel with Tahini Sauce
- Kale Caesar Salad
- Chia Seed Pudding
- Raw Berry Crumble
- Spiralized Beet Salad
- Mango Coconut Smoothie Bowl
- Mediterranean Zucchini Boats
- Raw Tacos with Walnut Meat
- Watermelon Gazpacho
- Sweet Potato Noodles with Almond Sauce
- Tomato Basil Zoodles
- Raw Banana Ice Cream
- Pineapple Cucumber Salad
- Green Smoothie
- Raw Spring Rolls with Peanut Dipping Sauce
- Broccoli Almond Salad
- Avocado Cacao Smoothie
- Raw Vegan Sushi Rolls
- Spicy Almond Nori Chips
- Chocolate Chia Seed Pudding
- Bell Pepper Nachos

- Raw Corn Chowder
- Mango Coconut Energy Bites
- Raw Pizza with Cashew Cheese
- Cucumber Avocado Soup
- Beetroot Hummus
- Tropical Fruit Salad
- Raw Apple Pie
- Rainbow Detox Salad
- Blueberry Spinach Smoothie
- Raw Chocolate Truffles
- Carrot Cake Bites
- Green Goddess Smoothie Bowl
- Raw Vegan Cheesecake
- Tomato Basil Zucchini Pasta
- Superfood Salad with Lemon Tahini Dressing

Green Goddess Salad

Ingredients:

For the Salad:

- 4 cups mixed salad greens (such as lettuce, spinach, arugula, and kale)
- 1 cucumber, thinly sliced
- 1 avocado, sliced
- 1 cup cherry tomatoes, halved
- 1/4 cup sliced radishes
- 1/4 cup sliced green onions
- 1/4 cup fresh parsley leaves
- 1/4 cup fresh basil leaves
- 1/4 cup fresh cilantro leaves
- 1/4 cup fresh tarragon leaves (optional)
- 1/4 cup toasted pine nuts or walnuts (optional)

For the Dressing:

- 1/2 cup plain Greek yogurt
- 1/4 cup mayonnaise
- 2 tablespoons chopped fresh parsley
- 2 tablespoons chopped fresh basil
- 2 tablespoons chopped fresh chives
- 1 tablespoon chopped fresh tarragon (optional)
- 1 tablespoon chopped fresh cilantro
- 2 cloves garlic, minced
- 2 tablespoons lemon juice
- Salt and pepper, to taste

Instructions:

1. Prepare the Salad Ingredients:
    1. Wash and dry the mixed salad greens, cucumber, cherry tomatoes, radishes, green onions, and herbs.
    2. Slice the cucumber, avocado, radishes, and green onions. Halve the cherry tomatoes.
    3. Tear the parsley, basil, cilantro, and tarragon leaves into smaller pieces if they are large.

4. Optional: Toast the pine nuts or walnuts in a dry skillet over medium heat until lightly golden and fragrant. Remove from heat and set aside to cool.

2. Make the Dressing:

    1. In a blender or food processor, combine the Greek yogurt, mayonnaise, chopped parsley, basil, chives, tarragon, cilantro, minced garlic, and lemon juice.
    2. Blend until the herbs are finely chopped and the dressing is smooth and creamy.
    3. Season the dressing with salt and pepper to taste. Adjust the seasoning as needed.

3. Assemble the Salad:

    1. In a large salad bowl, combine the mixed salad greens, sliced cucumber, avocado, cherry tomatoes, sliced radishes, sliced green onions, and torn herbs.
    2. Drizzle the prepared Green Goddess dressing over the salad ingredients, tossing gently to coat everything evenly.
    3. Sprinkle the toasted pine nuts or walnuts over the top of the salad, if using.

4. Serve and Enjoy:

    1. Serve the Green Goddess Salad immediately as a refreshing appetizer or side dish.
    2. Enjoy the vibrant colors and flavors of the fresh vegetables and herbs, paired with the creamy and herbaceous dressing.

Feel free to customize the Green Goddess Salad by adding other fresh vegetables such as bell peppers, carrots, or snap peas. You can also add protein such as grilled chicken, shrimp, or tofu to make it a more substantial meal. Enjoy this nutritious and delicious salad as part of a healthy lunch or dinner!

Zucchini Noodles with Pesto

Ingredients:

For the Pesto:

- 2 cups fresh basil leaves, packed
- 1/3 cup pine nuts or walnuts, toasted
- 1/3 cup grated Parmesan cheese
- 2 cloves garlic, peeled
- 1/2 cup extra virgin olive oil
- Salt and pepper, to taste

For the Zucchini Noodles:

- 4 medium zucchini
- 2 tablespoons olive oil
- Salt and pepper, to taste
- Grated Parmesan cheese, for garnish (optional)

Instructions:

1. Make the Pesto:

    1. In a food processor or blender, combine the fresh basil leaves, toasted pine nuts or walnuts, grated Parmesan cheese, and peeled garlic cloves.
    2. Pulse several times until the ingredients are finely chopped and well combined.
    3. With the food processor or blender running, slowly drizzle in the extra virgin olive oil until the pesto reaches your desired consistency.
    4. Season the pesto with salt and pepper to taste. Adjust the seasoning as needed.

2. Prepare the Zucchini Noodles:

    1. Using a spiralizer or julienne peeler, spiralize or julienne the zucchini into noodles.
    2. Heat 2 tablespoons of olive oil in a large skillet over medium heat.
    3. Add the zucchini noodles to the skillet and toss gently with tongs.
    4. Cook the zucchini noodles for 2-3 minutes, stirring occasionally, until they are just tender but still slightly crisp.
    5. Season the zucchini noodles with salt and pepper to taste.

3. Combine the Zucchini Noodles with Pesto:

1. Remove the skillet from the heat and add the homemade pesto to the zucchini noodles.
2. Toss the zucchini noodles with the pesto until they are evenly coated.
3. Taste and adjust the seasoning if necessary.

4. Serve and Garnish:

1. Transfer the zucchini noodles with pesto to serving plates or bowls.
2. Garnish with additional grated Parmesan cheese, if desired.
3. Serve immediately, while the zucchini noodles are still warm.

5. Enjoy:

1. Enjoy your zucchini noodles with pesto as a light and flavorful meal or side dish!
2. You can also add grilled chicken, shrimp, or cherry tomatoes to the zucchini noodles for extra protein and flavor, if desired.

This zucchini noodles with pesto recipe is not only delicious but also low in carbs and packed with nutrients. It's a great way to enjoy the flavors of pesto with a lighter twist using zucchini noodles instead of traditional pasta.

Raw Pad Thai

Ingredients:

For the Pad Thai Sauce:

- 1/4 cup almond butter (or peanut butter)
- 2 tablespoons tamari (or soy sauce)
- 2 tablespoons lime juice
- 1 tablespoon rice vinegar
- 1 tablespoon maple syrup (or honey)
- 1 clove garlic, minced
- 1 teaspoon grated ginger
- 1 teaspoon sriracha sauce (optional, for heat)
- 2-3 tablespoons water, to thin

For the Pad Thai:

- 2 medium zucchini, spiralized or julienned
- 2 large carrots, spiralized or julienned
- 1 red bell pepper, thinly sliced
- 1 cup bean sprouts
- 1/4 cup chopped cilantro
- 1/4 cup chopped green onions
- 1/4 cup chopped peanuts or cashews
- Lime wedges, for serving
- Optional: Additional toppings such as chopped fresh mint, basil, or sliced chili peppers

Instructions:

1. Make the Pad Thai Sauce:

   1. In a small bowl, whisk together almond butter, tamari (or soy sauce), lime juice, rice vinegar, maple syrup (or honey), minced garlic, grated ginger, and sriracha sauce (if using), until smooth.
   2. Add water, one tablespoon at a time, until the sauce reaches your desired consistency. Set aside.

2. Prepare the Vegetables:

1. Spiralize or julienne the zucchini and carrots into noodle-like strands using a spiralizer or julienne peeler.
2. Thinly slice the red bell pepper.
3. Rinse and drain the bean sprouts.
4. Chop the cilantro and green onions.
5. Chop the peanuts or cashews.

3. Assemble the Raw Pad Thai:

1. In a large mixing bowl, combine the spiralized zucchini and carrots, sliced red bell pepper, bean sprouts, chopped cilantro, and green onions.
2. Pour the Pad Thai sauce over the vegetables and toss gently until everything is evenly coated with the sauce.

4. Serve:

1. Divide the raw Pad Thai among serving plates or bowls.
2. Sprinkle chopped peanuts or cashews over the top of each serving.
3. Garnish with additional lime wedges and optional toppings such as chopped fresh mint, basil, or sliced chili peppers.
4. Serve immediately and enjoy!

5. Enjoy:

1. Enjoy your Raw Pad Thai as a light and refreshing meal or side dish, packed with fresh flavors and vibrant colors!
2. Feel free to customize the recipe by adding cooked protein such as grilled tofu, shrimp, or chicken if desired.

This Raw Pad Thai recipe is gluten-free, vegan, and raw, making it suitable for a variety of dietary preferences. It's perfect for a quick and healthy lunch or dinner, and you can easily customize it with your favorite vegetables and toppings.

Mango Salsa

Ingredients:

- 2 ripe mangoes, diced
- 1/2 red onion, finely chopped
- 1 red bell pepper, diced
- 1 jalapeño pepper, seeded and finely chopped (adjust to taste)
- 1/4 cup fresh cilantro, chopped
- Juice of 1 lime
- Salt and pepper, to taste

Optional Additions:

- 1 avocado, diced
- 1 small cucumber, diced
- 1/4 cup diced pineapple
- 1 tablespoon finely chopped fresh mint or basil
- Splash of hot sauce or chili flakes for extra heat

Instructions:

1. **Prepare the Ingredients:**
    - Peel the mangoes and dice them into small cubes.
    - Finely chop the red onion, red bell pepper, jalapeño pepper, and cilantro.
    - If using, dice the avocado and cucumber.
2. **Combine Ingredients:**
    - In a large mixing bowl, combine the diced mangoes, red onion, red bell pepper, jalapeño pepper, and cilantro.
    - If using, add the diced avocado, cucumber, and pineapple.
3. **Season:**
    - Squeeze the juice of one lime over the salsa.
    - Season with salt and pepper to taste.
    - If desired, add a splash of hot sauce or sprinkle of chili flakes for extra heat.
4. **Mix Well:**
    - Gently toss all the ingredients together until evenly combined.
5. **Chill (Optional):**

- If time allows, refrigerate the mango salsa for about 30 minutes to allow the flavors to meld together. This step is optional but can enhance the taste of the salsa.

6. **Serve:**
    - Once chilled (if desired), transfer the mango salsa to a serving bowl.
    - Garnish with additional cilantro leaves if desired.
    - Serve the mango salsa as a topping for grilled chicken, fish, shrimp, or tacos, or enjoy it as a dip with tortilla chips or alongside your favorite Mexican dishes.

7. **Enjoy!**
    - Enjoy the vibrant flavors of your homemade mango salsa! It's perfect for summer gatherings, BBQs, or as a quick and healthy snack. Adjust the ingredients according to your taste preferences and feel free to get creative with additional add-ins like diced pineapple or fresh herbs.

Coconut Curry Wraps

Ingredients:

For the Coconut Curry Filling:

- 1 tablespoon coconut oil
- 1 small onion, finely chopped
- 2 cloves garlic, minced
- 1 tablespoon fresh ginger, grated
- 2 tablespoons curry powder
- 1 can (14 oz) coconut milk
- 1 cup vegetable broth
- 2 cups mixed vegetables (such as bell peppers, carrots, broccoli, and snow peas), thinly sliced
- Salt and pepper to taste
- Fresh cilantro leaves, chopped (for garnish)

For the Wraps:

- Large flour tortillas or wraps
- Optional: Cooked rice or quinoa (for added texture and filling)

Instructions:

1. Prepare the Coconut Curry Filling:
    1. Heat coconut oil in a large skillet over medium heat.
    2. Add chopped onion and cook until softened, about 3-4 minutes.
    3. Stir in minced garlic and grated ginger, and cook for another 1-2 minutes until fragrant.
    4. Add curry powder to the skillet and cook, stirring constantly, for about 1 minute until aromatic.
    5. Pour in coconut milk and vegetable broth, and stir until well combined.
    6. Add mixed vegetables to the skillet and simmer for 8-10 minutes, or until the vegetables are tender and the sauce has thickened.
    7. Season with salt and pepper to taste. Adjust the seasoning if needed.
    8. Remove the skillet from heat and set aside.

2. Assemble the Coconut Curry Wraps:
    1. If using, lay a large flour tortilla or wrap on a flat surface.

2. Spoon a generous amount of the coconut curry filling onto the center of the tortilla.
3. Optional: Add a scoop of cooked rice or quinoa on top of the coconut curry filling for added texture and filling.
4. Sprinkle with chopped fresh cilantro leaves for garnish.
5. Fold the sides of the tortilla over the filling, then roll it up tightly to form a wrap.

3. Serve:

1. Slice the coconut curry wrap in half diagonally or serve whole.
2. Serve immediately while warm, or wrap tightly in foil for a portable lunch option.
3. Enjoy your delicious coconut curry wraps!

4. Variations:

- Add protein: Include cooked chicken, tofu, chickpeas, or shrimp to make the wraps more satisfying.
- Spice it up: Adjust the amount of curry powder or add red pepper flakes for extra heat.
- Customize the veggies: Use your favorite vegetables or whatever you have on hand. Spinach, mushrooms, and zucchini are also great additions.

These coconut curry wraps are versatile, customizable, and perfect for a quick and flavorful meal. They're also great for meal prep, as you can make a batch ahead of time and enjoy them throughout the week.

Rainbow Veggie Rolls

Ingredients:

For the Veggie Rolls:

- 8-10 rice paper wrappers
- 1 large carrot, julienned or thinly sliced
- 1 large cucumber, julienned or thinly sliced
- 1 bell pepper (red, yellow, or orange), thinly sliced
- 1 small red cabbage, thinly sliced
- 1 ripe mango, julienned or thinly sliced
- 1 avocado, thinly sliced
- Fresh cilantro leaves
- Fresh mint leaves
- Optional: Cooked rice noodles or vermicelli, for added texture

For the Dipping Sauce:

- 1/4 cup soy sauce or tamari
- 2 tablespoons rice vinegar
- 1 tablespoon honey or maple syrup
- 1 tablespoon lime juice
- 1 teaspoon grated ginger
- 1 clove garlic, minced
- Red pepper flakes, to taste (optional)
- Sesame seeds, for garnish (optional)

Instructions:

1. Prepare the Vegetables:

    1. Wash and prepare all the vegetables. Julienne or thinly slice the carrot, cucumber, bell pepper, red cabbage, mango, and avocado. Set aside.
    2. If using, cook rice noodles or vermicelli according to package instructions. Drain and set aside to cool.

2. Prepare the Dipping Sauce:

    1. In a small bowl, whisk together soy sauce or tamari, rice vinegar, honey or maple syrup, lime juice, grated ginger, minced garlic, and red pepper flakes (if using).
    2. Adjust the seasoning to taste and set aside.

3. Assemble the Veggie Rolls:

    1. Fill a shallow dish or pie plate with warm water.
    2. Dip one rice paper wrapper into the warm water for about 10-15 seconds until it becomes soft and pliable.
    3. Place the softened rice paper wrapper on a clean, damp kitchen towel or cutting board.
    4. Layer a small amount of each vegetable and herb filling (carrot, cucumber, bell pepper, red cabbage, mango, avocado, cilantro, mint, and cooked rice noodles if using) on the bottom third of the rice paper wrapper.
    5. Fold the bottom edge of the rice paper wrapper over the filling, then fold in the sides, and roll tightly to enclose the filling.
    6. Repeat with the remaining rice paper wrappers and filling ingredients.

4. Serve:

    1. Arrange the rainbow veggie rolls on a serving platter.
    2. Sprinkle with sesame seeds for garnish, if desired.
    3. Serve the veggie rolls with the prepared dipping sauce on the side.

5. Enjoy:

    1. Enjoy your colorful and nutritious rainbow veggie rolls as a light and refreshing meal or appetizer!
    2. These rolls are best enjoyed fresh, but you can store any leftovers in an airtight container in the refrigerator for up to one day. Note that rice paper wrappers may become slightly sticky if stored for too long.

Feel free to customize the veggie rolls with your favorite vegetables, herbs, or protein fillings. You can also try different dipping sauces or add a splash of sriracha for extra heat. Enjoy experimenting with different flavor combinations and creating your own vibrant rainbow veggie rolls!

Cashew Cheese Stuffed Peppers

Ingredients:

For the Cashew Cheese:

- 1 cup raw cashews, soaked in water for 4-6 hours or overnight
- 1/4 cup nutritional yeast
- 2 tablespoons lemon juice
- 1 clove garlic
- 1/2 teaspoon salt
- 1/4 teaspoon black pepper
- Water, as needed

For the Stuffed Peppers:

- 4 large bell peppers (any color), halved and seeds removed
- 1 cup cooked quinoa or rice
- 1 cup diced tomatoes
- 1/2 cup diced onion
- 1/2 cup diced zucchini
- 1/2 cup diced mushrooms
- 2 cloves garlic, minced
- 1 teaspoon olive oil
- Salt and pepper, to taste
- Fresh parsley or basil, chopped (for garnish)

Instructions:

1. Prepare the Cashew Cheese:
    1. Drain the soaked cashews and rinse them thoroughly.
    2. In a food processor or high-speed blender, combine the soaked cashews, nutritional yeast, lemon juice, garlic, salt, and black pepper.
    3. Blend until smooth and creamy, adding water as needed to achieve the desired consistency. Scrape down the sides of the blender or food processor as needed to ensure all ingredients are well incorporated.
    4. Taste and adjust seasoning if necessary. Set aside.

2. Prepare the Stuffed Peppers:
    1. Preheat the oven to 375°F (190°C). Line a baking sheet with parchment paper.

2. Heat olive oil in a skillet over medium heat. Add diced onion and garlic, and sauté until softened and fragrant, about 3-4 minutes.
3. Add diced zucchini and mushrooms to the skillet, and cook for an additional 3-4 minutes until tender.
4. Stir in cooked quinoa or rice and diced tomatoes, and cook for another 2-3 minutes until heated through. Season with salt and pepper to taste.
5. Fill each halved bell pepper with the quinoa and vegetable mixture, pressing down gently to pack it in.
6. Spoon cashew cheese over the top of each stuffed pepper, spreading it evenly with the back of a spoon.

3. Bake the Stuffed Peppers:

1. Place the stuffed peppers on the prepared baking sheet.
2. Cover the baking sheet with aluminum foil and bake in the preheated oven for 25-30 minutes, or until the peppers are tender and the filling is heated through.
3. Remove the foil during the last 10 minutes of baking to allow the cashew cheese to brown slightly.
4. Once done, remove the stuffed peppers from the oven and let them cool for a few minutes.
5. Garnish with chopped fresh parsley or basil before serving.

4. Serve:

1. Serve the cashew cheese stuffed peppers warm as a delicious main course or side dish.
2. Enjoy the creamy cashew cheese filling paired with the sweetness of the roasted peppers and flavorful quinoa and vegetable mixture.

These cashew cheese stuffed peppers are not only delicious but also vegan, gluten-free, and packed with nutrients. They make a great option for a healthy and satisfying meal that everyone will enjoy!

Beet and Avocado Carpaccio

Ingredients:

For the Beet Carpaccio:

- 2 medium-sized beets, peeled and thinly sliced
- 2 tablespoons olive oil
- 1 tablespoon balsamic vinegar
- Salt and pepper, to taste
- Optional: Fresh herbs (such as thyme or rosemary), for garnish

For the Avocado Carpaccio:

- 2 ripe avocados, peeled, pitted, and thinly sliced
- 1 tablespoon lemon juice
- Salt and pepper, to taste
- Optional: Red pepper flakes, for a hint of spice

For the Garnish:

- Fresh arugula or mixed greens
- Toasted nuts or seeds (such as pine nuts, walnuts, or pumpkin seeds)
- Crumbled goat cheese or feta cheese (optional, for added flavor)

Instructions:

1. Prepare the Beet Carpaccio:

    1. Preheat the oven to 400°F (200°C).
    2. Place the thinly sliced beets on a baking sheet lined with parchment paper.
    3. Drizzle olive oil and balsamic vinegar over the beet slices.
    4. Season with salt and pepper to taste.
    5. Roast the beets in the preheated oven for 15-20 minutes, or until tender.
    6. Remove from the oven and let cool slightly.

2. Prepare the Avocado Carpaccio:

    1. While the beets are roasting, prepare the avocado carpaccio.
    2. Thinly slice the ripe avocados and arrange them in a single layer on a serving platter.
    3. Drizzle lemon juice over the avocado slices to prevent browning.
    4. Season with salt and pepper to taste.

5. Optional: Sprinkle with red pepper flakes for a hint of spice.

3. Assemble the Carpaccio:

   1. Once the beets have cooled slightly, arrange them on top of the avocado slices on the serving platter.
   2. Alternate layers of beet slices and avocado slices until all are used.
   3. Optional: Garnish with fresh herbs, such as thyme or rosemary, for added flavor and visual appeal.

4. Serve:

   1. Serve the beet and avocado carpaccio on a bed of fresh arugula or mixed greens.
   2. Sprinkle with toasted nuts or seeds for added crunch and texture.
   3. Optional: Crumble goat cheese or feta cheese over the top for additional flavor.
   4. Drizzle with extra olive oil and balsamic vinegar, if desired.

5. Enjoy:

   1. Enjoy your beautiful and flavorful beet and avocado carpaccio as a light and refreshing appetizer or side dish!
   2. The combination of roasted beets and creamy avocado is sure to impress your guests and tantalize your taste buds.

This beet and avocado carpaccio is not only delicious but also nutritious, vegetarian, and gluten-free, making it a perfect option for a healthy and satisfying meal. Feel free to customize the recipe with your favorite herbs, nuts, and cheeses to suit your taste preferences.

Cucumber Gazpacho

Ingredients:

- 4 large cucumbers, peeled and chopped
- 1 green bell pepper, chopped
- 1 small red onion, chopped
- 2 cloves garlic, minced
- 2 tablespoons fresh lemon juice
- 2 tablespoons olive oil
- 1/4 cup fresh parsley leaves
- 1/4 cup fresh mint leaves
- 1 teaspoon salt, or to taste
- 1/2 teaspoon black pepper, or to taste
- 1 cup Greek yogurt (optional, for added creaminess)
- Additional cucumber slices, fresh herbs, and olive oil for garnish (optional)

Instructions:

1. Prepare the Ingredients:
    1. Peel and chop the cucumbers, and place them in a large bowl.
    2. Chop the green bell pepper, red onion, garlic, parsley, and mint, and add them to the bowl with the cucumbers.

2. Blend the Soup:
    1. In a blender or food processor, combine the chopped cucumbers, green bell pepper, red onion, garlic, lemon juice, olive oil, parsley, mint, salt, and black pepper.
    2. Blend until smooth and creamy. You may need to work in batches depending on the size of your blender or food processor.
    3. If using Greek yogurt, add it to the blender and blend until smooth and well combined.

3. Chill the Soup:
    1. Transfer the blended cucumber mixture to a large bowl or container.
    2. Cover and refrigerate the gazpacho for at least 1 hour to allow the flavors to meld together and the soup to chill thoroughly.

4. Serve:

1. Once chilled, give the gazpacho a stir and taste for seasoning, adjusting salt and pepper if needed.
2. Ladle the cucumber gazpacho into serving bowls.
3. Garnish each bowl with a drizzle of olive oil, a few cucumber slices, and fresh herbs, if desired.

5. Enjoy:

1. Serve the cucumber gazpacho immediately as a refreshing appetizer or light meal.
2. Enjoy its cool and refreshing flavors on a hot summer day!

This cucumber gazpacho is light, healthy, and bursting with fresh flavors. It's a great way to use up an abundance of cucumbers during the summer months and makes for a lovely starter for a backyard barbecue or picnic. Feel free to customize the recipe with additional herbs, spices, or other vegetables to suit your taste preferences.

Cauliflower Tabouli

Ingredients:

- 1 small head cauliflower, florets removed and finely chopped
- 2 cups fresh parsley leaves, finely chopped
- 1/2 cup fresh mint leaves, finely chopped
- 1/2 cup cherry tomatoes, quartered
- 1/4 cup red onion, finely chopped
- 1/4 cup cucumber, finely chopped
- 2 tablespoons lemon juice
- 2 tablespoons olive oil
- 1 clove garlic, minced
- Salt and pepper, to taste
- Optional: Crumbled feta cheese, olives, or chickpeas for added flavor and protein

Instructions:

1. Prepare the Cauliflower:
    1. Remove the florets from the cauliflower and discard the stems.
    2. Chop the cauliflower florets into small pieces. You can use a food processor to pulse the cauliflower until it resembles rice-like grains, or simply finely chop it with a knife.

2. Combine Ingredients:
    1. In a large mixing bowl, combine the finely chopped cauliflower, parsley, mint, cherry tomatoes, red onion, and cucumber.
    2. Toss the ingredients together until well mixed.

3. Make the Dressing:
    1. In a small bowl, whisk together the lemon juice, olive oil, minced garlic, salt, and pepper.
    2. Pour the dressing over the cauliflower tabouli mixture.

4. Mix Well:
    1. Gently toss the cauliflower tabouli until the vegetables are evenly coated with the dressing.
    2. Taste and adjust the seasoning, adding more salt, pepper, or lemon juice as needed.

5. Chill (Optional):

    1. Cover the cauliflower tabouli and refrigerate for at least 30 minutes to allow the flavors to meld together.
    2. This step is optional but recommended for best flavor.

6. Serve:

    1. Once chilled, give the cauliflower tabouli a final toss.
    2. Transfer to a serving bowl and garnish with additional fresh herbs, if desired.
    3. Optional: Add crumbled feta cheese, olives, or chickpeas for extra flavor and protein.
    4. Serve the cauliflower tabouli as a side dish, salad, or light meal.

7. Enjoy:

    1. Enjoy your delicious and healthy cauliflower tabouli!
    2. It's perfect for picnics, potlucks, or as a light and refreshing dish any time of the year.

This cauliflower tabouli is gluten-free, low-carb, and packed with fresh flavors and nutrients. It's a great way to incorporate more vegetables into your diet and can be easily customized with your favorite herbs, vegetables, and toppings.

Almond Butter Energy Balls

Ingredients:

- 1 cup rolled oats
- 1/2 cup almond butter
- 1/4 cup honey or maple syrup
- 1/4 cup unsweetened shredded coconut
- 1/4 cup ground flaxseed or chia seeds
- 1 teaspoon vanilla extract
- Pinch of salt
- Optional add-ins: chopped nuts, chocolate chips, dried fruit, cinnamon

Instructions:

1. Combine Ingredients: In a large mixing bowl, combine rolled oats, almond butter, honey or maple syrup, shredded coconut, ground flaxseed or chia seeds, vanilla extract, and a pinch of salt. Stir until well combined.
2. Mix Add-ins: If using any optional add-ins such as chopped nuts, chocolate chips, dried fruit, or cinnamon, add them to the mixture and stir until evenly distributed.
3. Chill Dough: Place the mixture in the refrigerator for 15-30 minutes to firm up slightly. Chilling the dough will make it easier to roll into balls.
4. Roll into Balls: Once chilled, remove the mixture from the refrigerator. Using your hands, scoop out small portions of the dough and roll them into balls about 1 inch in diameter. Repeat until all the mixture is used.
5. Store: Place the almond butter energy balls on a baking sheet lined with parchment paper or in an airtight container. If desired, you can roll the energy balls in additional shredded coconut or ground nuts for extra coating.
6. Chill: Store the almond butter energy balls in the refrigerator for at least 30 minutes to set.
7. Serve: Once set, the energy balls are ready to enjoy! They can be stored in an airtight container in the refrigerator for up to two weeks. They're perfect for a quick snack on the go, a pre-workout boost, or a sweet treat any time of the day.

Feel free to customize the recipe according to your taste preferences and dietary needs. You can swap almond butter for peanut butter or another nut butter, and adjust the sweetness level by adding more or less honey or maple syrup. Experiment with different add-ins to create your favorite flavor combinations!

Sprouted Quinoa Salad

Ingredients:

For the Salad:

- 1 cup sprouted quinoa (you can sprout it yourself or purchase pre-sprouted quinoa)
- 1 cup cherry tomatoes, halved
- 1 cucumber, diced
- 1 bell pepper, diced (any color)
- 1/4 cup red onion, finely chopped
- 1/4 cup fresh parsley, chopped
- 1/4 cup fresh cilantro, chopped
- 1/4 cup fresh mint leaves, chopped
- 1/4 cup toasted nuts or seeds (such as almonds, walnuts, sunflower seeds, or pumpkin seeds)
- Optional: 1/4 cup crumbled feta cheese or diced avocado for extra creaminess

For the Dressing:

- 1/4 cup extra virgin olive oil
- 2 tablespoons lemon juice or apple cider vinegar
- 1 clove garlic, minced
- 1 teaspoon Dijon mustard
- 1 teaspoon honey or maple syrup (optional)
- Salt and pepper, to taste

Instructions:

1. Cook the Sprouted Quinoa:

    1. Rinse the sprouted quinoa under cold water to remove any residue.
    2. In a medium saucepan, bring 2 cups of water to a boil.
    3. Add the rinsed sprouted quinoa to the boiling water.
    4. Reduce the heat to low, cover, and simmer for 15-20 minutes, or until the quinoa is tender and the water is absorbed.
    5. Remove from heat and let it cool.

2. Prepare the Salad Ingredients:

    1. While the quinoa is cooking, prepare the salad ingredients.

2. Chop the cherry tomatoes, cucumber, bell pepper, red onion, parsley, cilantro, and mint.
3. If using, toast the nuts or seeds in a dry skillet over medium heat until lightly golden and fragrant. Let them cool.

3. Make the Dressing:
    1. In a small bowl, whisk together the extra virgin olive oil, lemon juice or apple cider vinegar, minced garlic, Dijon mustard, honey or maple syrup (if using), salt, and pepper.
    2. Adjust the seasoning to taste, adding more lemon juice or vinegar if desired.

4. Assemble the Salad:
    1. In a large mixing bowl, combine the cooked and cooled sprouted quinoa with the chopped vegetables, herbs, and toasted nuts or seeds.
    2. If using, add the crumbled feta cheese or diced avocado to the salad.
    3. Drizzle the dressing over the salad and toss gently to coat all the ingredients evenly.

5. Serve:
    1. Transfer the sprouted quinoa salad to a serving dish or individual plates.
    2. Garnish with additional fresh herbs or a sprinkle of toasted nuts or seeds, if desired.
    3. Serve immediately, or refrigerate for 30 minutes to allow the flavors to meld together before serving.

6. Enjoy:
    1. Enjoy your nutritious and flavorful sprouted quinoa salad as a light and satisfying meal or side dish!
    2. This salad is perfect for picnics, potlucks, or meal prep, as it can be made ahead of time and stored in the refrigerator for up to three days.

Feel free to customize the salad with your favorite vegetables, herbs, nuts, and seeds. You can also add cooked chickpeas, grilled chicken, or tofu for added protein. Enjoy experimenting with different flavor combinations and creating your own delicious sprouted quinoa salad!

Raw Chocolate Avocado Mousse

Ingredients:

- 2 ripe avocados
- 1/4 cup cocoa powder
- 1/4 cup honey or maple syrup (adjust to taste)
- 1 teaspoon vanilla extract
- Pinch of salt
- Optional toppings: fresh berries, shaved chocolate, chopped nuts, coconut flakes

Instructions:

1. Prepare the Avocados: Cut the avocados in half, remove the pits, and scoop the flesh into a food processor or blender.
2. Blend Ingredients: Add the cocoa powder, honey or maple syrup, vanilla extract, and a pinch of salt to the food processor or blender with the avocados.
3. Blend Until Smooth: Blend the ingredients until smooth and creamy, scraping down the sides of the food processor or blender as needed to ensure everything is well combined.
4. Taste and Adjust: Taste the mousse and adjust the sweetness if necessary by adding more honey or maple syrup, if desired.
5. Chill (Optional): For a thicker consistency, transfer the mousse to a bowl and refrigerate for 30 minutes to 1 hour before serving. This also allows the flavors to meld together.
6. Serve: Divide the chocolate avocado mousse into serving bowls or glasses. You can top it with fresh berries, shaved chocolate, chopped nuts, or coconut flakes for added flavor and texture.
7. Enjoy: Serve the raw chocolate avocado mousse immediately and enjoy its rich, creamy texture and decadent chocolate flavor!

This raw chocolate avocado mousse is not only delicious but also healthy and packed with nutrients from the avocados. It's a great alternative to traditional dairy-based mousses and makes a satisfying dessert for any occasion. Plus, it's quick and easy to make, requiring just a few simple ingredients and minimal prep time. Give it a try for a guilt-free indulgence!

Carrot Ginger Soup

Ingredients:

- 1 tablespoon olive oil or coconut oil
- 1 onion, chopped
- 2 cloves garlic, minced
- 1 tablespoon fresh ginger, grated
- 1 pound carrots, peeled and chopped
- 4 cups vegetable broth
- 1 (14-ounce) can coconut milk
- Salt and pepper, to taste
- Optional toppings: chopped fresh cilantro, toasted pumpkin seeds, a drizzle of coconut milk

Instructions:

1. Sauté Aromatics: In a large pot or Dutch oven, heat the olive oil over medium heat. Add the chopped onion and sauté for 5-7 minutes, or until softened and translucent. Add the minced garlic and grated ginger, and cook for an additional 1-2 minutes, until fragrant.
2. Add Carrots: Add the chopped carrots to the pot, and stir to combine with the onion, garlic, and ginger.
3. Simmer: Pour the vegetable broth into the pot, covering the carrots and aromatics. Bring the mixture to a boil, then reduce the heat to low and simmer, covered, for 20-25 minutes, or until the carrots are tender and easily pierced with a fork.
4. Blend: Once the carrots are cooked through, remove the pot from the heat. Using an immersion blender, blend the soup until smooth and creamy. Alternatively, carefully transfer the soup in batches to a blender and blend until smooth.
5. Add Coconut Milk: Return the blended soup to the pot (if using a blender), and stir in the coconut milk until well combined. Season with salt and pepper, to taste.
6. Adjust Consistency: If the soup is too thick, you can add more vegetable broth or water until you reach your desired consistency.
7. Reheat: Place the pot back on the stove over low heat to warm the soup through, stirring occasionally.
8. Serve: Ladle the carrot ginger soup into bowls. Garnish with chopped fresh cilantro, toasted pumpkin seeds, and a drizzle of coconut milk, if desired.

9. Enjoy: Serve the carrot ginger soup hot and enjoy its comforting and warming flavors!

This carrot ginger soup is not only delicious but also nutritious, vegan, and gluten-free. It's perfect for a cozy weeknight dinner or as a starter for a special meal. The combination of sweet carrots and spicy ginger creates a balanced and flavorful soup that's sure to become a new favorite!

Raw Falafel with Tahini Sauce

Ingredients:

For the Raw Falafel:

- 1 cup raw almonds
- 1 cup raw walnuts
- 1 cup fresh parsley, chopped
- 1 cup fresh cilantro, chopped
- 3 cloves garlic
- 1 teaspoon ground cumin
- 1 teaspoon ground coriander
- 1/2 teaspoon ground turmeric
- 1/4 teaspoon cayenne pepper (optional, for heat)
- Juice of 1 lemon
- Salt and pepper, to taste

For the Tahini Sauce:

- 1/2 cup tahini
- Juice of 1 lemon
- 2 cloves garlic, minced
- 1/4 cup water (or more, as needed)
- Salt, to taste

Optional toppings:

- Chopped fresh parsley or cilantro
- Diced tomatoes
- Sliced cucumber
- Pickled vegetables
- Pita bread or lettuce leaves, for serving

Instructions:

1. Prepare the Raw Falafel:

    1. In a food processor, combine the raw almonds and walnuts. Pulse until finely ground.

2. Add the chopped parsley, cilantro, garlic, ground cumin, ground coriander, ground turmeric, cayenne pepper (if using), lemon juice, salt, and pepper to the food processor.
3. Pulse until the mixture comes together and forms a coarse paste. Be careful not to over-process; you want the mixture to have some texture.
4. Taste the mixture and adjust seasoning as needed.

2. Form the Falafel:

   1. Using your hands, shape the falafel mixture into small patties or balls, about 1 inch in diameter.
   2. Place the formed falafel on a plate or baking sheet lined with parchment paper. Refrigerate for at least 30 minutes to firm up.

3. Make the Tahini Sauce:

   1. In a small bowl, whisk together the tahini, lemon juice, minced garlic, and water until smooth.
   2. Add more water as needed to achieve your desired consistency. The sauce should be creamy and pourable.
   3. Season with salt, to taste.

4. Serve:

   1. Arrange the raw falafel on a serving platter.
   2. Drizzle the tahini sauce over the falafel.
   3. Garnish with chopped fresh parsley or cilantro, if desired.
   4. Serve with optional toppings such as diced tomatoes, sliced cucumber, pickled vegetables, and pita bread or lettuce leaves.

5. Enjoy:

   1. Enjoy your delicious raw falafel with tahini sauce as a light and nutritious meal or snack!
   2. These raw falafel are packed with flavor and make a great addition to any meal.

This raw falafel with tahini sauce recipe is vegan, gluten-free, and loaded with nutrients from the nuts, herbs, and spices. It's a perfect option for a healthy and satisfying dish that's sure to please everyone at the table!

Kale Caesar Salad

Ingredients:

For the Salad:

- 1 bunch kale (about 8-10 ounces), stems removed and leaves torn into bite-sized pieces
- 1/2 cup croutons (store-bought or homemade)
- 1/4 cup shaved or grated Parmesan cheese
- Optional: cooked chicken breast or grilled shrimp for protein

For the Caesar Dressing:

- 1/4 cup mayonnaise
- 2 tablespoons freshly squeezed lemon juice
- 2 tablespoons grated Parmesan cheese
- 1 tablespoon Dijon mustard
- 1 clove garlic, minced
- 2 anchovy fillets, minced (optional)
- 1/4 cup extra virgin olive oil
- Salt and pepper, to taste

Instructions:

1. Prepare the Kale:

    1. Wash the kale leaves thoroughly under cold water and pat them dry with paper towels.
    2. Remove the tough stems from the kale leaves and discard them. Tear the leaves into bite-sized pieces and place them in a large salad bowl.

2. Make the Caesar Dressing:

    1. In a small bowl, whisk together the mayonnaise, lemon juice, grated Parmesan cheese, Dijon mustard, minced garlic, and minced anchovy fillets (if using).
    2. Slowly drizzle in the extra virgin olive oil while whisking continuously until the dressing is smooth and well combined.
    3. Season the dressing with salt and pepper, to taste. Adjust the seasoning if necessary.

3. Dress the Salad:

1. Pour the Caesar dressing over the torn kale leaves in the salad bowl.
2. Use clean hands or salad tongs to massage the dressing into the kale leaves. Massaging the kale helps to tenderize it and infuse it with flavor.
3. Continue massaging the kale for 2-3 minutes, or until it begins to soften and wilt slightly.

4. Assemble the Salad:

    1. Add the croutons and shaved or grated Parmesan cheese to the salad bowl with the dressed kale.
    2. Toss the salad gently to combine all the ingredients and evenly distribute the dressing.
    3. If desired, add cooked chicken breast or grilled shrimp to the salad for added protein.

5. Serve:

    1. Divide the kale Caesar salad among individual plates or bowls.
    2. Optionally, garnish with additional shaved or grated Parmesan cheese and freshly ground black pepper.
    3. Serve immediately and enjoy your delicious and nutritious kale Caesar salad!

This kale Caesar salad is packed with flavor and texture, making it a satisfying meal or side dish. The hearty kale leaves hold up well to the creamy Caesar dressing, while the croutons add a crunchy contrast. Feel free to customize the salad with your favorite toppings and protein options for a delicious and healthy meal!

Chia Seed Pudding

Ingredients:

- 1/4 cup chia seeds
- 1 cup milk of your choice (almond milk, coconut milk, cow's milk, etc.)
- 1-2 tablespoons sweetener of your choice (honey, maple syrup, agave nectar, etc.)
- 1/2 teaspoon vanilla extract (optional)
- Optional toppings: fresh fruit, nuts, seeds, coconut flakes, granola, etc.

Instructions:

1. Combine Chia Seeds and Liquid:

    1. In a mixing bowl or jar, combine the chia seeds, milk, sweetener of your choice, and vanilla extract (if using). Stir well to combine.

2. Let it Sit:

    1. Once the ingredients are mixed, cover the bowl or jar and let it sit in the refrigerator for at least 2 hours, or preferably overnight. During this time, the chia seeds will absorb the liquid and swell, creating a thick pudding-like consistency.

3. Stir Occasionally:

    1. After the first hour, give the chia seed mixture a stir to prevent clumping and ensure even distribution of the seeds.

4. Check Consistency:

    1. After the soaking time is complete, check the consistency of the chia seed pudding. If it's too thick for your liking, you can stir in a little more milk to thin it out.

5. Serve:

    1. Once the chia seed pudding reaches your desired consistency, it's ready to serve.
    2. Divide the pudding into individual serving bowls or jars.
    3. Optionally, top the pudding with your favorite toppings, such as fresh fruit, nuts, seeds, coconut flakes, or granola.

6. Enjoy:

1. Enjoy your homemade chia seed pudding as a nutritious and delicious breakfast, snack, or dessert!
2. Store any leftover pudding in an airtight container in the refrigerator for up to 3-4 days.

This basic recipe for chia seed pudding is customizable to suit your taste preferences. You can adjust the sweetness, flavorings, and toppings to create endless variations of this healthy and satisfying treat. Experiment with different types of milk, sweeteners, and flavorings to discover your favorite combination!

Raw Berry Crumble

Ingredients:

For the Berry Filling:

- 4 cups mixed fresh berries (such as strawberries, blueberries, raspberries, blackberries)
- 2 tablespoons maple syrup or honey (adjust to taste)
- 1 tablespoon lemon juice
- 1 teaspoon vanilla extract
- Pinch of salt

For the Crumble Topping:

- 1 cup rolled oats
- 1/2 cup almonds, walnuts, or pecans
- 1/4 cup shredded coconut (unsweetened)
- 2 tablespoons maple syrup or honey
- 2 tablespoons coconut oil, melted
- 1 teaspoon ground cinnamon
- Pinch of salt

Instructions:

1. Prepare the Berry Filling:

    1. Wash the fresh berries and pat them dry with paper towels. If using strawberries, hull and slice them.
    2. In a mixing bowl, combine the fresh berries with maple syrup or honey, lemon juice, vanilla extract, and a pinch of salt. Stir gently to coat the berries evenly. Set aside while you prepare the crumble topping.

2. Make the Crumble Topping:

    1. In a food processor, combine the rolled oats, nuts, shredded coconut, maple syrup or honey, melted coconut oil, ground cinnamon, and a pinch of salt.
    2. Pulse the mixture several times until it resembles coarse crumbs and sticks together when pressed between your fingers. Be careful not to over-process; you want some texture remaining.

3. Assemble the Crumble:

1. Spread the prepared berry filling evenly in the bottom of a serving dish or individual ramekins.
2. Sprinkle the crumble topping evenly over the berry filling, covering it completely.

4. Chill (Optional):

1. For best results, refrigerate the raw berry crumble for at least 30 minutes to allow the flavors to meld together and the topping to firm up slightly.

5. Serve:

1. Once chilled, remove the raw berry crumble from the refrigerator.
2. Serve it as is or with a dollop of yogurt or whipped coconut cream on top.
3. Optionally, garnish with fresh mint leaves or additional berries before serving.

6. Enjoy:

1. Enjoy your delicious and healthy raw berry crumble as a refreshing dessert or snack!
2. Store any leftovers in the refrigerator for up to 2-3 days.

This raw berry crumble is packed with flavor and nutrients from the fresh berries and nuts. It's naturally sweetened with maple syrup or honey and doesn't require any baking, making it a quick and easy dessert option for any occasion. Feel free to customize the recipe with your favorite berries and nuts for endless variations!

Spiralized Beet Salad

Ingredients:

For the Salad:

- 2 medium-sized beets, peeled
- 2 cups mixed greens (such as spinach, arugula, or kale)
- 1/4 cup crumbled feta cheese or goat cheese
- 1/4 cup toasted walnuts or pecans, chopped
- 2 tablespoons dried cranberries or golden raisins

For the Dressing:

- 2 tablespoons extra virgin olive oil
- 1 tablespoon balsamic vinegar
- 1 teaspoon honey or maple syrup
- 1 teaspoon Dijon mustard
- Salt and pepper, to taste

Optional Additions:

- Sliced avocado
- Cooked quinoa or farro
- Grilled chicken or tofu
- Fresh herbs (such as parsley or cilantro)

Instructions:

1. Spiralize the Beets:
    1. Using a spiralizer, spiralize the peeled beets into thin noodle-like strands.
    2. Alternatively, you can use a julienne peeler or mandoline slicer to create thin strips of beets.

2. Prepare the Dressing:
    1. In a small bowl, whisk together the extra virgin olive oil, balsamic vinegar, honey or maple syrup, Dijon mustard, salt, and pepper until well combined. Set aside.

3. Assemble the Salad:

1. In a large mixing bowl, combine the spiralized beets, mixed greens, crumbled feta or goat cheese, chopped toasted nuts, and dried cranberries or golden raisins.
2. If using any optional additions such as sliced avocado, cooked grains, or protein, add them to the salad bowl as well.

4. Dress the Salad:

1. Drizzle the prepared dressing over the salad ingredients in the mixing bowl.
2. Toss gently to coat all the ingredients evenly with the dressing.

5. Serve:

1. Transfer the dressed spiralized beet salad to serving plates or bowls.
2. Optionally, garnish with additional toasted nuts, crumbled cheese, or fresh herbs before serving.

6. Enjoy:

1. Enjoy your colorful and nutritious spiralized beet salad as a refreshing side dish or light meal!
2. Serve it as is, or pair it with grilled protein or whole grains for a more substantial meal.

This spiralized beet salad is packed with flavor, texture, and nutrients, making it a satisfying and healthy option for any occasion. The combination of sweet beets, tangy dressing, creamy cheese, and crunchy nuts creates a delightful flavor and texture contrast that's sure to impress. Feel free to customize the salad with your favorite ingredients and enjoy its vibrant colors and fresh flavors!

Mango Coconut Smoothie Bowl

Ingredients:

For the Smoothie Base:

- 1 ripe mango, peeled, pitted, and chopped (or 1 cup frozen mango chunks)
- 1/2 cup coconut milk (from a can or carton)
- 1/2 cup plain Greek yogurt or coconut yogurt
- 1 ripe banana, peeled and frozen
- 1/2 cup ice cubes (optional, for a thicker consistency)
- 1 tablespoon honey or maple syrup (optional, for added sweetness)
- 1/2 teaspoon vanilla extract (optional, for flavor)

For Toppings (Optional):

- Fresh mango slices
- Toasted coconut flakes
- Granola
- Chia seeds or hemp seeds
- Sliced bananas
- Fresh berries (such as strawberries, blueberries, or raspberries)
- Nut butter (such as almond butter or peanut butter)

Instructions:

1. Prepare the Smoothie Base:
    1. In a blender, combine the chopped mango, coconut milk, Greek yogurt or coconut yogurt, frozen banana, ice cubes (if using), honey or maple syrup (if using), and vanilla extract (if using).
    2. Blend until smooth and creamy, scraping down the sides of the blender as needed to ensure all ingredients are well combined. If the smoothie is too thick, you can add more coconut milk or a splash of water to reach your desired consistency.

2. Serve the Smoothie Bowl:
    1. Pour the smoothie base into serving bowls.
    2. Use a spoon to smooth the surface of the smoothie base evenly in each bowl.

3. Add Toppings:

1. Arrange your desired toppings on top of the smoothie base. You can get creative and arrange the toppings in rows or clusters for a visually appealing presentation.
2. Some popular toppings for mango coconut smoothie bowls include fresh mango slices, toasted coconut flakes, granola, chia seeds or hemp seeds, sliced bananas, fresh berries, and a drizzle of nut butter.

4. Enjoy:

1. Enjoy your delicious mango coconut smoothie bowl immediately!
2. Use a spoon to scoop up some of the smoothie base along with the toppings for a satisfying and nutritious breakfast or snack.

This mango coconut smoothie bowl is not only tasty but also packed with vitamins, minerals, and healthy fats from the mango, coconut milk, yogurt, and toppings. It's a great way to start your day on a refreshing note or enjoy as a mid-day pick-me-up! Feel free to customize the smoothie base and toppings to suit your taste preferences and dietary needs.

Mediterranean Zucchini Boats

Ingredients:

- 4 medium zucchini
- 1 tablespoon olive oil
- 1 small onion, finely chopped
- 2 cloves garlic, minced
- 1 bell pepper, diced (red, yellow, or orange)
- 1 cup cherry tomatoes, halved
- 1/2 cup crumbled feta cheese
- 1/4 cup chopped fresh basil leaves
- 1/4 cup chopped fresh parsley leaves
- 1/4 cup pitted Kalamata olives, chopped
- Salt and pepper, to taste
- Optional: cooked quinoa, rice, or lentils for added protein and texture

Instructions:

1. Preheat the Oven:

    1. Preheat your oven to 375°F (190°C).

2. Prepare the Zucchini:

    1. Wash the zucchini thoroughly and pat them dry with paper towels.
    2. Trim the stem ends of the zucchini and cut them in half lengthwise.
    3. Use a spoon to scoop out the seeds and flesh from the center of each zucchini half, creating a hollowed-out "boat." Leave about 1/4 inch of flesh around the edges to create a sturdy boat.

3. Prepare the Filling:

    1. In a large skillet, heat the olive oil over medium heat.
    2. Add the chopped onion and minced garlic to the skillet. Cook, stirring occasionally, until the onion is translucent and fragrant, about 3-4 minutes.
    3. Add the diced bell pepper to the skillet and cook for an additional 2-3 minutes, until slightly softened.
    4. Stir in the cherry tomatoes and cook for another 2 minutes, just until they start to soften.
    5. Remove the skillet from the heat and stir in the crumbled feta cheese, chopped basil, chopped parsley, and chopped Kalamata olives. Season with salt and

pepper, to taste. If using cooked quinoa, rice, or lentils, stir them into the filling mixture as well.

4. Assemble and Bake the Zucchini Boats:
   1. Place the hollowed-out zucchini boats in a baking dish, cut side up.
   2. Spoon the filling mixture evenly into each zucchini boat, pressing it down gently to pack it in.
   3. Cover the baking dish with foil and bake in the preheated oven for 20-25 minutes, or until the zucchini is tender and the filling is heated through.

5. Serve:
   1. Once the zucchini boats are done baking, remove them from the oven.
   2. Serve the Mediterranean zucchini boats hot, garnished with additional chopped fresh herbs or a sprinkle of crumbled feta cheese, if desired.

6. Enjoy:
   1. Enjoy your flavorful and nutritious Mediterranean zucchini boats as a delicious main dish or side dish!

These Mediterranean zucchini boats are packed with vibrant colors, flavors, and textures, making them a satisfying and healthy meal option. Feel free to customize the filling with your favorite Mediterranean ingredients and enjoy this dish as a vegetarian entree or as part of a Mediterranean-inspired feast!

Raw Tacos with Walnut Meat

Ingredients:

For the Walnut Meat:

- 1 cup raw walnuts
- 1 tablespoon tamari or soy sauce
- 1 tablespoon olive oil
- 1 teaspoon chili powder
- 1/2 teaspoon ground cumin
- 1/2 teaspoon smoked paprika
- 1/4 teaspoon garlic powder
- Pinch of cayenne pepper (optional, for heat)
- Salt and pepper, to taste

For the Taco Assembly:

- Large lettuce leaves or cabbage leaves (such as romaine lettuce or iceberg lettuce)
- Toppings of your choice: diced tomatoes, sliced avocado, shredded carrots, chopped red onion, cilantro, salsa, lime wedges, etc.

Instructions:

1. Prepare the Walnut Meat:

   1. In a food processor, combine the raw walnuts, tamari or soy sauce, olive oil, chili powder, ground cumin, smoked paprika, garlic powder, cayenne pepper (if using), salt, and pepper.
   2. Pulse the mixture several times until the walnuts are finely chopped and resemble the texture of ground meat. Be careful not to over-process; you want some texture remaining.

2. Assemble the Tacos:

   1. Wash and dry the large lettuce leaves or cabbage leaves, then pat them dry with paper towels.
   2. Place a spoonful of the walnut meat mixture onto each lettuce leaf, spreading it out evenly.

3. Top the walnut meat with your desired taco toppings, such as diced tomatoes, sliced avocado, shredded carrots, chopped red onion, cilantro, salsa, and a squeeze of lime juice.

3. Serve:

1. Arrange the assembled raw tacos on a serving platter.
2. Serve immediately and enjoy your delicious raw tacos with walnut meat!

These raw tacos with walnut meat are packed with flavor, protein, and healthy fats, making them a satisfying and nutritious meal option. They're also gluten-free, dairy-free, and vegan, making them suitable for a variety of dietary preferences. Feel free to customize the taco toppings to suit your taste preferences and enjoy this fresh and flavorful dish any time of day!

Watermelon Gazpacho

Ingredients:

- 4 cups seedless watermelon, diced
- 2 large tomatoes, diced
- 1 cucumber, peeled, seeded, and diced
- 1 red bell pepper, diced
- 1/2 red onion, diced
- 2 cloves garlic, minced
- 1/4 cup fresh basil leaves
- 1/4 cup fresh mint leaves
- 2 tablespoons fresh lime juice
- 2 tablespoons extra virgin olive oil
- 1 tablespoon red wine vinegar
- Salt and pepper, to taste
- Optional garnishes: diced avocado, crumbled feta cheese, chopped fresh herbs, drizzle of balsamic glaze

Instructions:

1. Prepare the Ingredients:

    1. Wash and dice the seedless watermelon, tomatoes, cucumber, red bell pepper, red onion, garlic, basil leaves, and mint leaves.
    2. If using, peel and seed the cucumber before dicing it.

2. Blend the Soup:

    1. In a blender or food processor, combine the diced watermelon, tomatoes, cucumber, red bell pepper, red onion, garlic, basil leaves, mint leaves, lime juice, olive oil, and red wine vinegar.
    2. Blend the mixture until smooth and creamy. You may need to blend in batches depending on the size of your blender or food processor.

3. Season to Taste:

    1. Taste the gazpacho and season with salt and pepper, to taste. Adjust the seasoning as needed.

4. Chill the Soup:

    1. Transfer the blended gazpacho to a large bowl or pitcher.

2. Cover and refrigerate the gazpacho for at least 1-2 hours, or until thoroughly chilled.

5. Serve:
   1. Once chilled, give the gazpacho a stir to mix any separation that may have occurred.
   2. Ladle the chilled watermelon gazpacho into serving bowls or glasses.
   3. Garnish each serving with diced avocado, crumbled feta cheese, chopped fresh herbs, and a drizzle of balsamic glaze, if desired.

6. Enjoy:
   1. Serve the watermelon gazpacho immediately as a refreshing appetizer or light meal.
   2. Enjoy its vibrant flavors and cooling properties on a hot summer day!

This watermelon gazpacho is a perfect balance of sweet, tangy, and savory flavors, with a refreshing and hydrating quality that's ideal for warm weather. It's also packed with vitamins, minerals, and antioxidants, making it a nutritious addition to your summer menu. Feel free to adjust the ingredients and seasonings to suit your taste preferences and enjoy this chilled soup all season long!

Sweet Potato Noodles with Almond Sauce

Ingredients:

For the Sweet Potato Noodles:

- 2 large sweet potatoes, peeled
- 2 tablespoons olive oil
- Salt and pepper, to taste

For the Almond Sauce:

- 1/2 cup almond butter
- 2 tablespoons soy sauce or tamari
- 2 tablespoons rice vinegar
- 1 tablespoon maple syrup or honey
- 1 clove garlic, minced
- 1 teaspoon grated ginger
- 1/4 cup water, or more as needed

Optional Toppings:

- Sliced green onions
- Sesame seeds
- Crushed red pepper flakes
- Chopped cilantro
- Sliced bell peppers
- Cooked protein of your choice (such as tofu, chicken, or shrimp)

Instructions:

1. Prepare the Sweet Potato Noodles:

    1. Using a spiralizer, spiralize the peeled sweet potatoes into noodle-like strands.
    2. Heat the olive oil in a large skillet over medium heat. Add the sweet potato noodles to the skillet and sauté for 5-7 minutes, or until the noodles are tender but still slightly crisp.
    3. Season the noodles with salt and pepper, to taste. Remove from heat and set aside.

2. Make the Almond Sauce:

1. In a small bowl, whisk together the almond butter, soy sauce or tamari, rice vinegar, maple syrup or honey, minced garlic, grated ginger, and water until smooth and creamy. Add more water as needed to reach your desired consistency.

3. Assemble the Dish:

    1. Pour the almond sauce over the cooked sweet potato noodles in the skillet.
    2. Toss the noodles gently to coat them evenly with the sauce.
    3. If desired, add any optional toppings such as sliced green onions, sesame seeds, crushed red pepper flakes, chopped cilantro, sliced bell peppers, or cooked protein of your choice.

4. Serve:

    1. Once everything is well combined and heated through, remove the skillet from the heat.
    2. Divide the sweet potato noodles with almond sauce among serving plates or bowls.
    3. Optionally, garnish with additional toppings before serving.

5. Enjoy:

    1. Enjoy your delicious sweet potato noodles with almond sauce as a satisfying and nutritious meal!
    2. Serve immediately and savor the creamy texture and flavorful combination of ingredients.

This sweet potato noodles with almond sauce dish is not only tasty but also packed with vitamins, minerals, and healthy fats from the sweet potatoes and almonds. It's a great way to enjoy a healthy and satisfying meal that's gluten-free, dairy-free, and vegan-friendly. Feel free to customize the dish with your favorite toppings and enjoy it as a quick and easy weeknight dinner or meal prep option!

Tomato Basil Zoodles

Ingredients:

For the Tomato Basil Sauce:

- 2 tablespoons olive oil
- 2 cloves garlic, minced
- 1 (14 oz) can diced tomatoes
- 1 teaspoon dried basil (or 2 tablespoons fresh basil, chopped)
- Salt and pepper, to taste
- Pinch of red pepper flakes (optional, for heat)

For the Zoodles:

- 4 medium zucchini, spiralized
- Salt, to taste

Optional Garnish:

- Grated Parmesan cheese
- Fresh basil leaves
- Crushed red pepper flakes

Instructions:

1. Prepare the Tomato Basil Sauce:

   1. In a large skillet, heat the olive oil over medium heat. Add the minced garlic and sauté for 1-2 minutes, until fragrant.
   2. Add the diced tomatoes (with their juices) to the skillet. Stir in the dried basil, salt, pepper, and red pepper flakes (if using).
   3. Simmer the sauce for 8-10 minutes, stirring occasionally, until it thickens slightly. Taste and adjust seasoning if needed.

2. Cook the Zoodles:

   1. While the sauce is simmering, spiralize the zucchini into noodle-like strands using a spiralizer.
   2. Place the spiralized zucchini noodles in a colander set over a bowl or in the sink. Sprinkle with salt and toss to coat. Let the zoodles sit for about 10 minutes to release excess moisture.

3. After 10 minutes, use your hands to squeeze out any excess moisture from the zucchini noodles. This will prevent the final dish from becoming watery.

3. Combine the Zoodles and Sauce:

    1. Once the sauce has thickened and the excess moisture has been removed from the zucchini noodles, add the spiralized zucchini to the skillet with the tomato basil sauce.
    2. Toss the zoodles gently with the sauce until they are evenly coated and heated through. Be careful not to overcook the zoodles, as they should remain crisp-tender.

4. Serve:

    1. Divide the tomato basil zoodles among serving plates.
    2. Garnish with grated Parmesan cheese, fresh basil leaves, and crushed red pepper flakes, if desired.

5. Enjoy:

    1. Serve the tomato basil zoodles immediately as a light and delicious meal!
    2. Enjoy the fresh flavors of the zucchini noodles paired with the savory tomato basil sauce.

This tomato basil zoodles recipe is a quick and easy way to enjoy a healthy and low-carb meal that's packed with flavor. It's perfect for a light lunch or dinner, and you can customize it with your favorite toppings or protein additions if desired. Enjoy!

Raw Banana Ice Cream

Ingredients:

- 4 ripe bananas, peeled, sliced, and frozen
- Optional add-ins or flavorings:
    - 1-2 tablespoons unsweetened cocoa powder (for chocolate banana ice cream)
    - 1 teaspoon vanilla extract
    - 1/4 cup peanut butter or almond butter
    - Fresh berries or sliced fruit
    - Nuts or chocolate chips for topping

Instructions:

1. Freeze the Bananas:

    1. Peel ripe bananas and slice them into coins.
    2. Place the banana slices in a single layer on a baking sheet lined with parchment paper or a silicone mat.
    3. Place the baking sheet in the freezer and freeze the banana slices for at least 2-3 hours, or until completely frozen.

2. Make the Raw Banana Ice Cream:

    1. Once the banana slices are frozen solid, transfer them to a food processor or high-speed blender.
    2. If using any optional add-ins or flavorings (such as cocoa powder, vanilla extract, or nut butter), add them to the food processor or blender with the frozen banana slices.
    3. Process or blend the frozen banana slices until smooth and creamy, scraping down the sides of the container as needed. This may take a few minutes and require periodic pausing to scrape down the sides and break up any clumps.
    4. If the mixture is too thick and difficult to blend, you can add a splash of non-dairy milk (such as almond milk or coconut milk) to help it blend more easily. Be careful not to add too much liquid, as you want the ice cream to be thick and creamy.

3. Serve:

    1. Once the raw banana ice cream is smooth and creamy, transfer it to serving bowls or cones.

2. Garnish with your favorite toppings, such as fresh berries, sliced fruit, nuts, or chocolate chips.

4. Enjoy:
    1. Serve the raw banana ice cream immediately as a refreshing and guilt-free treat!
    2. Enjoy its creamy texture and natural sweetness, knowing that it's made entirely from wholesome ingredients.

This raw banana ice cream is a delicious and nutritious alternative to traditional dairy ice cream. It's perfect for those with dietary restrictions or anyone looking for a lighter dessert option. Experiment with different flavor variations and toppings to create your own custom creations!

Pineapple Cucumber Salad

Ingredients:

- 2 cups fresh pineapple chunks
- 1 large cucumber, peeled and diced
- 1/4 cup red onion, thinly sliced (optional)
- 2 tablespoons fresh cilantro or mint leaves, chopped
- Juice of 1 lime
- 1 tablespoon honey or maple syrup (optional, for added sweetness)
- Salt, to taste
- Crushed red pepper flakes or chili powder (optional, for a hint of spice)

Instructions:

1. Prepare the Ingredients:

    1. Peel and dice the cucumber into bite-sized pieces.
    2. If using fresh pineapple, remove the skin and core, then cut the pineapple into chunks. If using canned pineapple, drain the pineapple chunks from the can.

2. Combine the Ingredients:

    1. In a large mixing bowl, combine the pineapple chunks, diced cucumber, thinly sliced red onion (if using), and chopped cilantro or mint leaves.
    2. Toss the ingredients gently to combine.

3. Add the Dressing:

    1. Drizzle the lime juice over the pineapple and cucumber mixture.
    2. If desired, drizzle honey or maple syrup over the salad to add a touch of sweetness.
    3. Season with a pinch of salt to enhance the flavors.
    4. Optionally, sprinkle crushed red pepper flakes or chili powder over the salad for a hint of spice.

4. Toss and Chill:

    1. Gently toss the pineapple cucumber salad until all the ingredients are evenly coated with the dressing.
    2. Cover the salad bowl with plastic wrap or a lid and refrigerate for at least 30 minutes to allow the flavors to meld together and the salad to chill.

5. Serve:

    1. Once chilled, give the pineapple cucumber salad a final toss.
    2. Serve the salad in individual bowls or on a serving platter, garnished with additional chopped cilantro or mint leaves if desired.

6. Enjoy:

    1. Serve the pineapple cucumber salad as a refreshing side dish or light appetizer!
    2. Enjoy its crisp and juicy flavors, perfect for a hot summer day or any time you crave something light and refreshing.

This pineapple cucumber salad is not only delicious but also packed with vitamins, minerals, and antioxidants, making it a nutritious addition to your meal. Feel free to customize the salad with your favorite herbs, spices, or additional ingredients such as bell peppers, cherry tomatoes, or avocado. Enjoy!

Green Smoothie

Ingredients:

- 1 cup spinach or kale leaves, tightly packed
- 1 ripe banana, fresh or frozen
- 1/2 cup fresh or frozen mixed berries (such as strawberries, blueberries, or raspberries)
- 1/2 cup plain Greek yogurt or dairy-free yogurt alternative
- 1/2 cup almond milk, coconut milk, or any other milk of your choice
- 1 tablespoon chia seeds or flaxseeds (optional, for added fiber and omega-3 fatty acids)
- 1 tablespoon honey or maple syrup (optional, for added sweetness)
- Ice cubes (if not using frozen fruits)

Instructions:

1. Prepare the Ingredients:
    1. Wash the spinach or kale leaves thoroughly and remove any tough stems.
    2. Peel the banana and slice it into chunks if it's not already frozen.
    3. If using fresh berries, wash them under running water and remove any stems or leaves.

2. Blend the Smoothie:
    1. In a blender, combine the spinach or kale leaves, banana chunks, mixed berries, Greek yogurt or yogurt alternative, almond milk or other milk, and chia seeds or flaxseeds (if using).
    2. If desired, add honey or maple syrup for added sweetness.
    3. Blend the ingredients on high speed until smooth and creamy. If the smoothie is too thick, you can add more milk or a splash of water to reach your desired consistency.
    4. If using fresh fruits instead of frozen, you can add a handful of ice cubes to the blender to make the smoothie cold and refreshing.

3. Serve:
    1. Once the green smoothie is blended to your liking, pour it into glasses.
    2. Optionally, garnish each smoothie with a sprinkle of chia seeds, flaxseeds, or fresh berries for added texture and visual appeal.

4. Enjoy:

    1. Serve the green smoothie immediately as a nutritious and energizing breakfast, snack, or post-workout drink!
    2. Sip and enjoy the refreshing flavors while reaping the health benefits of the leafy greens, fruits, and other nutritious ingredients.

This basic green smoothie recipe is highly customizable, so feel free to adjust the ingredients and proportions to suit your taste preferences and dietary needs. You can also experiment with different combinations of fruits, greens, and add-ins such as protein powder, nut butters, or coconut water to create your own signature green smoothie recipe. Enjoy!

Raw Spring Rolls with Peanut Dipping Sauce

Ingredients:

For the Spring Rolls:

- 8 rice paper wrappers
- 2 cups mixed salad greens or lettuce leaves
- 1 large carrot, julienned or grated
- 1 cucumber, julienned
- 1 red bell pepper, thinly sliced
- 1/2 cup fresh mint leaves
- 1/2 cup fresh cilantro leaves
- 1/2 cup fresh basil leaves
- 1 avocado, thinly sliced (optional)
- Cooked protein of your choice, such as shrimp, chicken, or tofu (optional)

For the Peanut Dipping Sauce:

- 1/4 cup smooth peanut butter
- 2 tablespoons soy sauce or tamari
- 2 tablespoons lime juice
- 2 tablespoons water
- 1 tablespoon maple syrup or honey
- 1 teaspoon grated ginger
- 1 clove garlic, minced
- Crushed red pepper flakes, to taste (optional)
- Chopped peanuts, for garnish (optional)

Instructions:

1. Prepare the Ingredients:

   1. Wash and prepare all the vegetables, herbs, and protein (if using). Julienne or thinly slice the carrots, cucumber, and bell pepper. Tear the salad greens into bite-sized pieces. Slice the avocado, if using.
   2. Prepare a clean work surface for assembling the spring rolls, such as a large cutting board or damp kitchen towel.

2. Soften the Rice Paper Wrappers:

   1. Fill a shallow dish or pie plate with warm water.

2. Working with one rice paper wrapper at a time, dip the wrapper into the warm water for about 10-15 seconds, or until it becomes soft and pliable. Be careful not to over-soak the wrapper, as it will become too fragile to work with.
3. Place the softened wrapper onto your work surface.

3. Assemble the Spring Rolls:

   1. Place a small handful of salad greens or lettuce leaves in the center of the rice paper wrapper, leaving some space around the edges.
   2. Layer the julienned carrots, cucumber, and bell pepper on top of the greens.
   3. Add a few leaves each of mint, cilantro, and basil.
   4. If using avocado or cooked protein, add a few slices or pieces on top of the vegetables.
   5. Fold the bottom edge of the rice paper wrapper over the filling, then fold in the sides, and roll tightly to enclose the filling, similar to rolling a burrito.
   6. Repeat the process with the remaining rice paper wrappers and filling ingredients.

4. Make the Peanut Dipping Sauce:

   1. In a small bowl, whisk together the peanut butter, soy sauce or tamari, lime juice, water, maple syrup or honey, grated ginger, minced garlic, and crushed red pepper flakes (if using) until smooth and well combined.
   2. If the sauce is too thick, you can add more water, 1 tablespoon at a time, until you reach your desired consistency.

5. Serve:

   1. Arrange the assembled spring rolls on a serving platter.
   2. Garnish with chopped peanuts, if desired.
   3. Serve the spring rolls with the peanut dipping sauce on the side for dipping.

6. Enjoy:

   1. Enjoy the fresh and flavorful raw spring rolls with peanut dipping sauce as a healthy appetizer, light meal, or snack!
   2. Dip the spring rolls in the creamy peanut sauce and savor the delicious combination of flavors and textures.

Feel free to customize the spring rolls with your favorite vegetables, herbs, and protein options. You can also adjust the dipping sauce to your taste preferences by adding more or less of the ingredients. Enjoy!

Broccoli Almond Salad

Ingredients:

For the Salad:

- 4 cups broccoli florets
- 1/2 cup sliced almonds, toasted
- 1/4 cup red onion, finely chopped (optional)
- 1/4 cup dried cranberries or raisins (optional)
- 1/4 cup crumbled feta cheese or grated Parmesan cheese (optional)

For the Dressing:

- 1/4 cup mayonnaise or Greek yogurt
- 2 tablespoons apple cider vinegar or white wine vinegar
- 1 tablespoon honey or maple syrup
- 1 tablespoon Dijon mustard
- Salt and pepper, to taste

Instructions:

1. Prepare the Broccoli:

    1. Wash the broccoli thoroughly under cold running water. Cut the broccoli into bite-sized florets, discarding any tough stems.

2. Toast the Almonds:

    1. In a dry skillet over medium heat, toast the sliced almonds, stirring frequently, until golden brown and fragrant, about 3-5 minutes. Be careful not to burn them. Remove from heat and let cool.

3. Make the Dressing:

    1. In a small bowl, whisk together the mayonnaise or Greek yogurt, apple cider vinegar or white wine vinegar, honey or maple syrup, Dijon mustard, salt, and pepper until smooth and well combined. Adjust seasoning to taste.

4. Assemble the Salad:

    1. In a large mixing bowl, combine the broccoli florets, toasted sliced almonds, chopped red onion (if using), and dried cranberries or raisins (if using).

2. Pour the dressing over the broccoli mixture and toss until the ingredients are evenly coated with the dressing.
3. If using, sprinkle crumbled feta cheese or grated Parmesan cheese over the salad and gently toss to incorporate.

5. Chill and Serve:

1. Cover the bowl with plastic wrap or a lid and refrigerate the broccoli almond salad for at least 30 minutes to allow the flavors to meld together and the salad to chill.
2. Once chilled, give the salad a final toss and adjust seasoning if necessary.
3. Serve the broccoli almond salad chilled as a side dish or light meal.

6. Enjoy:

1. Enjoy the crisp texture and delicious flavors of the broccoli almond salad!
2. Serve alongside grilled chicken, fish, or as part of a picnic or potluck spread.

This broccoli almond salad is versatile and can be customized with your favorite ingredients. Feel free to add other vegetables such as cherry tomatoes, bell peppers, or shredded carrots, or substitute the almonds with toasted walnuts or pecans. Enjoy!

Avocado Cacao Smoothie

Ingredients:

- 1 ripe avocado, peeled and pitted
- 2 tablespoons cacao powder (unsweetened)
- 1 tablespoon honey or maple syrup (optional, for added sweetness)
- 1 cup milk of your choice (such as almond milk, coconut milk, or dairy milk)
- 1/2 teaspoon vanilla extract
- Ice cubes, as needed

Instructions:

1. Prepare the Ingredients:
    1. Cut the avocado in half, remove the pit, and scoop out the flesh into a blender.
2. Add the Remaining Ingredients:
    1. To the blender, add the cacao powder, honey or maple syrup (if using), milk of your choice, and vanilla extract.
3. Blend Until Smooth:
    1. Blend the ingredients on high speed until smooth and creamy. If the smoothie is too thick, you can add more milk or a splash of water to reach your desired consistency.
    2. If desired, add a few ice cubes to the blender and blend again until the smoothie is chilled.
4. Taste and Adjust:
    1. Taste the smoothie and adjust the sweetness if necessary by adding more honey or maple syrup.
    2. You can also adjust the thickness of the smoothie by adding more milk if desired.
5. Serve:
    1. Once the avocado cacao smoothie is blended to your liking, pour it into glasses.
    2. Optionally, garnish with a sprinkle of cacao powder or a few slices of avocado for presentation.
6. Enjoy:

1. Serve the avocado cacao smoothie immediately as a delicious and nutritious beverage!
2. Sip and enjoy the creamy texture and rich chocolatey flavor of the smoothie.

This avocado cacao smoothie is not only delicious but also packed with healthy fats, antioxidants, and nutrients from the avocado and cacao powder. It's perfect for a quick and easy breakfast, snack, or post-workout refuel. Feel free to customize the smoothie with your favorite toppings or add-ins, such as banana, nut butter, or protein powder. Enjoy!

Raw Vegan Sushi Rolls

Ingredients:

For the Sushi Rice:

- 1 cup cauliflower florets
- 1 tablespoon rice vinegar
- 1 teaspoon maple syrup or agave syrup
- Pinch of salt

For the Fillings:

- Nori seaweed sheets
- Assorted vegetables (such as cucumber, avocado, carrot, bell pepper, and lettuce), thinly sliced or julienned
- Fresh herbs (such as cilantro, mint, or basil)
- Optional add-ins: tofu, tempeh, or marinated mushrooms

For the Dipping Sauce (optional):

- Soy sauce or tamari
- Wasabi paste
- Pickled ginger

Instructions:

1. Prepare the Sushi Rice:
    1. In a food processor, pulse the cauliflower florets until they resemble rice-like grains.
    2. Transfer the cauliflower rice to a clean kitchen towel or nut milk bag and squeeze out any excess moisture.
    3. In a bowl, combine the cauliflower rice with rice vinegar, maple syrup or agave syrup, and a pinch of salt. Mix well to combine.

2. Assemble the Sushi Rolls:
    1. Lay a sheet of nori seaweed shiny side down on a sushi rolling mat or a clean kitchen towel.
    2. Spread a thin layer of cauliflower rice evenly over the nori, leaving about an inch of space at the top edge.

3. Arrange your choice of sliced vegetables, herbs, and optional add-ins horizontally across the center of the cauliflower rice.

3. Roll the Sushi:
    1. Using the sushi rolling mat or kitchen towel, tightly roll the nori and filling into a cylinder, starting from the bottom edge.
    2. Apply gentle pressure to compress the roll as you roll it up.
    3. Moisten the top edge of the nori with a little water to seal the roll.
    4. Repeat the process with the remaining nori sheets and filling ingredients.

4. Slice and Serve:
    1. Using a sharp knife, slice each sushi roll into bite-sized pieces.
    2. Arrange the sushi rolls on a serving platter and serve with soy sauce or tamari, wasabi paste, and pickled ginger on the side for dipping.

5. Enjoy:
    1. Enjoy your homemade raw vegan sushi rolls as a nutritious and delicious meal or snack!
    2. Get creative with different fillings and variations to suit your taste preferences.

These raw vegan sushi rolls are not only healthy and satisfying but also customizable and fun to make. Experiment with different vegetables, herbs, and sauces to create your own unique sushi creations. Enjoy!

Spicy Almond Nori Chips

Ingredients:

- Nori sheets (seaweed sheets)
- Almonds (whole or sliced)
- Olive oil or sesame oil
- Spices (such as chili powder, paprika, cayenne pepper, or any other spice blend you prefer)
- Salt to taste

Instructions:

1. Preheat your oven to around 300°F (150°C).
2. Cut the nori sheets into smaller chip-sized squares or rectangles. You can use scissors for this.
3. In a bowl, mix the almonds with a bit of olive oil or sesame oil until they are lightly coated.
4. Add your desired spices to the almonds. If you like it really spicy, don't be shy with the chili powder or cayenne pepper!
5. Lay the nori squares on a baking sheet lined with parchment paper.
6. Place a seasoned almond on each nori square.
7. Lightly sprinkle some salt over the top of each chip.
8. Bake in the preheated oven for about 10-15 minutes, or until the nori becomes crisp and the almonds are roasted. Keep an eye on them to prevent burning.
9. Once done, remove from the oven and let them cool slightly before serving.

These Spicy Almond Nori Chips are sure to be a hit at any gathering or as a tasty snack for yourself! Enjoy the crunchy, savory, and spicy flavors all in one bite.

Chocolate Chia Seed Pudding

Ingredients:

- 1/4 cup chia seeds
- 1 cup milk (dairy or plant-based)
- 2-3 tablespoons cocoa powder (unsweetened)
- 1-2 tablespoons honey or maple syrup (adjust to taste)
- 1/2 teaspoon vanilla extract
- Optional toppings: fresh berries, sliced bananas, shredded coconut, chopped nuts, or whipped cream

Instructions:

1. In a bowl, whisk together the milk, cocoa powder, honey or maple syrup, and vanilla extract until well combined and smooth.
2. Add the chia seeds to the mixture and whisk again to evenly distribute the seeds.
3. Let the mixture sit for about 5-10 minutes, then whisk again to prevent clumping.
4. Cover the bowl and refrigerate for at least 2 hours, or preferably overnight, to allow the chia seeds to absorb the liquid and thicken into a pudding-like consistency.
5. After the pudding has chilled and thickened, give it a good stir. If it's too thick, you can add a bit more milk to reach your desired consistency.
6. Divide the chocolate chia seed pudding into serving dishes or jars.
7. Top with your favorite toppings, such as fresh berries, sliced bananas, shredded coconut, chopped nuts, or a dollop of whipped cream.
8. Serve chilled and enjoy this delicious and nutritious Chocolate Chia Seed Pudding!

This pudding is not only tasty but also packed with fiber, protein, and healthy fats from the chia seeds, making it a satisfying and guilt-free dessert or snack option.

Bell Pepper Nachos

Ingredients:

- Bell peppers (any color you prefer)
- Ground beef or turkey (cooked and seasoned with taco seasoning)
- Black beans (drained and rinsed)
- Corn kernels (fresh or canned)
- Shredded cheese (cheddar, Monterey Jack, or a Mexican blend)
- Optional toppings: diced tomatoes, sliced jalapeños, sliced olives, diced onions, chopped cilantro, sour cream, guacamole, salsa

Instructions:

1. Preheat your oven to 375°F (190°C).
2. Wash the bell peppers and slice them in half lengthwise. Remove the seeds and membranes to create pepper halves that can hold the nacho toppings.
3. Place the pepper halves on a baking sheet lined with parchment paper or aluminum foil, cut side up.
4. Fill each pepper half with a layer of cooked ground beef or turkey.
5. Add a spoonful of black beans and corn kernels on top of the meat.
6. Sprinkle shredded cheese over the peppers, covering the toppings.
7. Place the baking sheet in the preheated oven and bake for about 10-15 minutes, or until the cheese is melted and bubbly, and the peppers are tender but still slightly crisp.
8. Once done, remove the bell pepper nachos from the oven and let them cool for a few minutes.
9. Top the nachos with your favorite toppings, such as diced tomatoes, sliced jalapeños, sliced olives, diced onions, chopped cilantro, sour cream, guacamole, or salsa.
10. Serve the bell pepper nachos warm and enjoy this tasty and nutritious twist on nachos!

These bell pepper nachos are not only flavorful and satisfying but also packed with vitamins and nutrients from the bell peppers and other wholesome ingredients. They make a great appetizer, snack, or even a light meal. Feel free to customize the toppings to suit your taste preferences!

Raw Corn Chowder

Ingredients:

- 4 ears of corn, kernels removed (about 3 cups)
- 1 cup chopped tomatoes
- 1/2 cup diced red bell pepper
- 1/2 cup diced cucumber
- 1/4 cup diced red onion
- 2 cloves garlic, minced
- 2 cups vegetable broth (or more as needed for desired consistency)
- 1/4 cup fresh cilantro, chopped
- 2 tablespoons lime juice
- 1 tablespoon olive oil
- Salt and pepper to taste
- Optional toppings: diced avocado, chopped scallions, a dollop of Greek yogurt or sour cream, extra cilantro

Instructions:

1. In a blender or food processor, combine the corn kernels, chopped tomatoes, diced red bell pepper, diced cucumber, minced garlic, vegetable broth, lime juice, and olive oil.
2. Blend until smooth and creamy. You may need to do this in batches depending on the size of your blender or food processor.
3. If you prefer a chunkier texture, reserve some of the corn kernels, tomatoes, bell pepper, and cucumber and stir them into the blended mixture.
4. Season the chowder with salt and pepper to taste. Adjust the consistency by adding more vegetable broth if desired.
5. Transfer the raw corn chowder to serving bowls.
6. Stir in the chopped cilantro for added freshness.
7. Serve the chowder chilled or at room temperature.
8. Garnish with optional toppings such as diced avocado, chopped scallions, a dollop of Greek yogurt or sour cream, and extra cilantro.
9. Enjoy this vibrant and flavorful Raw Corn Chowder as a light meal or appetizer!

This raw corn chowder is packed with the natural sweetness of fresh corn and the refreshing flavors of tomatoes, bell peppers, cucumber, and cilantro. It's a perfect dish to enjoy during the summer months when corn is in season. Feel free to adjust the seasonings and toppings according to your taste preferences.

Mango Coconut Energy Bites

Ingredients:

- 1 cup dried mango (unsweetened)
- 1 cup shredded coconut (unsweetened)
- 1/2 cup rolled oats
- 1/4 cup almonds or cashews
- 2 tablespoons honey or maple syrup
- 1 tablespoon coconut oil
- 1/2 teaspoon vanilla extract
- Pinch of salt (optional)

Instructions:

1. In a food processor, combine the dried mango, shredded coconut, rolled oats, and almonds or cashews.
2. Pulse the ingredients until they are finely chopped and well combined.
3. Add the honey or maple syrup, coconut oil, vanilla extract, and a pinch of salt (if using) to the mixture in the food processor.
4. Pulse again until the mixture starts to come together and forms a sticky dough. If the mixture seems too dry, you can add a little more honey or maple syrup.
5. Once the mixture is well combined and sticky, use your hands to roll it into small balls, about 1 inch in diameter.
6. Place the energy bites on a baking sheet lined with parchment paper.
7. Optional: Roll the energy bites in additional shredded coconut for extra coating.
8. Chill the energy bites in the refrigerator for at least 30 minutes to firm up.
9. Once chilled, transfer the mango coconut energy bites to an airtight container for storage.
10. Enjoy these delicious and nutritious snacks whenever you need a quick boost of energy!

These Mango Coconut Energy Bites are packed with natural sweetness from the mango and a satisfying crunch from the coconut and nuts. They're perfect for snacking between meals, pre- or post-workout, or whenever you need a little pick-me-up during the day. Plus, they're customizable, so feel free to add your favorite nuts, seeds, or spices to suit your taste preferences.

Raw Pizza with Cashew Cheese

Ingredients:

For the crust:

- 2 cups raw almonds
- 1 cup sunflower seeds
- 1/2 cup ground flaxseed
- 2 tablespoons nutritional yeast
- 1 teaspoon dried oregano
- 1 teaspoon dried basil
- 1/2 teaspoon garlic powder
- Pinch of sea salt
- Water, as needed

For the cashew cheese:

- 1 1/2 cups raw cashews (soaked in water for at least 2 hours, then drained)
- 1/4 cup nutritional yeast
- 2 tablespoons lemon juice
- 1 tablespoon apple cider vinegar
- 1 clove garlic
- 1/2 teaspoon sea salt
- Water, as needed

For the toppings:

- Sliced tomatoes
- Sliced bell peppers
- Sliced onions
- Sliced mushrooms
- Fresh basil leaves
- Any other toppings of your choice

Instructions:

1. Prepare the crust:
   - In a food processor, combine the almonds, sunflower seeds, ground flaxseed, nutritional yeast, dried oregano, dried basil, garlic powder, and a pinch of sea salt.
   - Pulse until the mixture resembles coarse crumbs.
   - With the food processor running, slowly add water a little at a time until the mixture begins to stick together and forms a dough-like consistency.
   - Transfer the dough to a piece of parchment paper and use your hands to press it into a round crust shape, about 1/4 inch thick.
2. Prepare the cashew cheese:
   - In a blender, combine the soaked and drained cashews, nutritional yeast, lemon juice, apple cider vinegar, garlic, and sea salt.
   - Blend until smooth and creamy, adding water as needed to achieve your desired consistency. The cheese should be thick but spreadable.
3. Assemble the pizza:
   - Spread a generous layer of the cashew cheese evenly over the prepared crust.
   - Arrange your desired toppings over the cheese. Get creative and layer them however you like!
   - Garnish with fresh basil leaves for extra flavor.
4. Serve:
   - Once assembled, slice the raw pizza into wedges and serve immediately.
   - Enjoy the delicious and nutritious flavors of your homemade raw pizza with cashew cheese!

Feel free to experiment with different toppings and flavor combinations to suit your taste preferences. Raw pizza is versatile and can be customized to include your favorite vegetables and herbs.

Cucumber Avocado Soup

Ingredients:

- 2 large cucumbers, peeled and diced
- 1 ripe avocado, peeled and pitted
- 1/4 cup fresh cilantro leaves
- 1/4 cup fresh mint leaves
- 1 clove garlic, minced
- 2 green onions, chopped
- 2 cups vegetable broth (or more for desired consistency)
- 1/4 cup plain Greek yogurt (optional, for added creaminess)
- Juice of 1 lime
- Salt and pepper to taste
- Optional garnishes: diced cucumber, chopped fresh herbs, a drizzle of olive oil, a dollop of Greek yogurt

Instructions:

1. Prepare the ingredients:
    - Peel and dice the cucumbers.
    - Peel and pit the avocado.
    - Mince the garlic.
    - Chop the cilantro, mint, and green onions.
2. Blend the soup:
    - In a blender or food processor, combine the diced cucumbers, avocado, cilantro, mint, garlic, green onions, vegetable broth, Greek yogurt (if using), and lime juice.
    - Blend until smooth and creamy. You may need to do this in batches depending on the size of your blender or food processor.
3. Adjust consistency and seasoning:
    - If the soup is too thick, you can add more vegetable broth to reach your desired consistency.
    - Season the soup with salt and pepper to taste. Adjust the seasoning as needed.
4. Chill the soup:
    - Transfer the blended soup to a bowl or container and cover it.
    - Chill in the refrigerator for at least 1 hour, or until thoroughly chilled.
5. Serve:

- Once chilled, give the soup a good stir.
- Ladle the cucumber avocado soup into serving bowls.
- Garnish with diced cucumber, chopped fresh herbs, a drizzle of olive oil, and a dollop of Greek yogurt, if desired.
- Serve immediately and enjoy this refreshing and nutritious chilled soup!

Cucumber Avocado Soup is perfect for serving as an appetizer or light meal on a hot day. It's packed with fresh flavors and creamy texture from the avocado, making it both delicious and satisfying. Feel free to adjust the ingredients and seasonings to suit your taste preferences.

Beetroot Hummus

Ingredients:

- 1 can (15 ounces) chickpeas, drained and rinsed
- 2 medium-sized cooked beetroots (about 1 cup), peeled and chopped
- 2 cloves garlic, minced
- 3 tablespoons tahini (sesame paste)
- 3 tablespoons fresh lemon juice
- 2 tablespoons olive oil
- 1/2 teaspoon ground cumin
- Salt and pepper to taste
- Water, as needed for consistency
- Optional garnishes: drizzle of olive oil, sprinkle of sesame seeds, chopped fresh herbs (such as parsley or cilantro)

Instructions:

1. Prepare the beetroots:
    - If you haven't already, cook the beetroots until tender. You can boil, steam, or roast them. Once cooked, allow them to cool slightly, then peel and chop them into chunks.
2. Blend the ingredients:
    - In a food processor or blender, combine the chickpeas, cooked beetroots, minced garlic, tahini, lemon juice, olive oil, ground cumin, salt, and pepper.
    - Blend until smooth and creamy, scraping down the sides of the processor or blender as needed. If the mixture is too thick, you can add a little water, a tablespoon at a time, until you reach your desired consistency.
3. Adjust seasoning:
    - Taste the beetroot hummus and adjust the seasoning as needed. You can add more lemon juice, salt, or cumin according to your taste preferences.
4. Serve:
    - Transfer the beetroot hummus to a serving bowl.
    - Drizzle with a little extra olive oil and sprinkle with sesame seeds or chopped fresh herbs for garnish, if desired.
5. Enjoy:
    - Serve the beetroot hummus with pita bread, crackers, vegetable sticks, or as a spread for sandwiches or wraps.

- Enjoy this vibrant and nutritious dip as a tasty snack or appetizer!

Beetroot hummus is not only delicious but also packed with nutrients and antioxidants from the chickpeas and beetroots. It's a great way to add some color and variety to your hummus repertoire, and it's sure to impress at parties or gatherings. Feel free to adjust the ingredients and seasonings to suit your taste preferences.

Tropical Fruit Salad

Ingredients:

- 2 cups pineapple chunks
- 2 cups mango chunks
- 2 cups papaya chunks
- 1 cup sliced strawberries
- 1 cup kiwi slices
- 1 cup grapes (halved if large)
- Juice of 1 lime
- 2 tablespoons honey or maple syrup (optional, for a sweeter salad)
- Fresh mint leaves for garnish (optional)

Instructions:

1. Prepare the fruits:
    - Wash and prepare all the fruits as needed. Peel and chop the pineapple, mango, and papaya into bite-sized chunks. Slice the strawberries and kiwi. If the grapes are large, you can halve them.
2. Combine the fruits:
    - In a large mixing bowl, combine all the prepared fruits.
3. Add the dressing:
    - Squeeze the juice of one lime over the fruit salad.
    - If you prefer a sweeter salad, you can drizzle honey or maple syrup over the fruits. Alternatively, you can omit the sweetener if the fruits are already sweet enough for your taste.
4. Gently toss:
    - Using a large spoon or spatula, gently toss the fruits and dressing together until they are well combined.
5. Chill:
    - Cover the fruit salad and place it in the refrigerator to chill for at least 30 minutes before serving. Chilling allows the flavors to meld together and enhances the overall taste of the salad.
6. Serve:
    - Once chilled, transfer the tropical fruit salad to a serving bowl or individual plates.

- Garnish with fresh mint leaves for a pop of color and extra freshness, if desired.
7. Enjoy:
    - Serve the tropical fruit salad as a refreshing snack, side dish, or dessert.
    - Enjoy the burst of tropical flavors and the natural sweetness of the fresh fruits!

This Tropical Fruit Salad is not only delicious but also packed with vitamins, minerals, and antioxidants from the assortment of fruits. It's a perfect dish to enjoy on a hot summer day or to brighten up any meal with its vibrant colors and flavors. Feel free to customize the fruit selection based on what's in season and your personal preferences.

Raw Apple Pie

Ingredients:

For the crust:

- 1 cup raw almonds
- 1 cup dates, pitted
- Pinch of salt

For the filling:

- 3-4 medium-sized apples, peeled and thinly sliced
- 1 tablespoon lemon juice
- 1 teaspoon ground cinnamon
- 1/4 teaspoon ground nutmeg
- 2 tablespoons maple syrup or honey (optional, depending on the sweetness of the apples)
- Pinch of salt

Instructions:

1. Prepare the crust:
    - In a food processor, combine the raw almonds, pitted dates, and a pinch of salt.
    - Pulse the ingredients until they are finely ground and begin to stick together.
    - Press the mixture firmly into the bottom of a pie dish to form the crust. Make sure it's evenly distributed and compacted.
2. Prepare the filling:
    - In a large bowl, toss the thinly sliced apples with lemon juice to prevent them from browning.
    - Add the ground cinnamon, ground nutmeg, maple syrup or honey (if using), and a pinch of salt. Toss until the apples are evenly coated.
3. Assemble the pie:

- Arrange the seasoned apple slices evenly over the prepared crust in the pie dish. You can layer them neatly or pile them on top, depending on your preference.
4. Chill:
    - Place the raw apple pie in the refrigerator to chill for at least 30 minutes before serving. Chilling allows the flavors to meld together and helps the pie hold its shape when sliced.
5. Serve:
    - Once chilled, slice the raw apple pie into wedges and serve.
    - Optionally, you can garnish each slice with a sprinkle of cinnamon or a drizzle of maple syrup for extra sweetness.
6. Enjoy:
    - Serve the raw apple pie as a delicious and healthy dessert option.
    - Enjoy the natural sweetness of the apples combined with the nutty crust for a satisfying treat!

This Raw Apple Pie is not only tasty but also packed with nutrients from the raw almonds and fresh apples. It's a great way to enjoy the flavors of apple pie without having to bake. Feel free to customize the recipe by adding your favorite spices or toppings, such as chopped nuts or a dollop of coconut cream.

Rainbow Detox Salad

Ingredients:

For the salad:

- 2 cups mixed salad greens (such as spinach, kale, or arugula)
- 1 medium carrot, grated
- 1 medium beetroot, grated
- 1/2 cup red cabbage, thinly sliced
- 1 bell pepper (any color), thinly sliced
- 1 cup cherry tomatoes, halved
- 1/2 cucumber, thinly sliced
- 1/2 cup shredded purple cabbage
- 1/4 cup red onion, thinly sliced
- 1/4 cup fresh parsley, chopped
- 1/4 cup almonds or walnuts, chopped (optional)
- Optional additions: avocado slices, cooked quinoa, cooked chickpeas, or any other veggies of your choice

For the dressing:

- 1/4 cup olive oil
- 2 tablespoons apple cider vinegar or lemon juice
- 1 tablespoon honey or maple syrup
- 1 teaspoon Dijon mustard
- 1 clove garlic, minced
- Salt and pepper to taste

Instructions:

1. Prepare the salad ingredients:
    - Wash and prepare all the vegetables as needed. Grate the carrot and beetroot, thinly slice the red cabbage, bell pepper, cucumber, and red onion. Halve the cherry tomatoes. Chop the fresh parsley.
2. Assemble the salad:

- In a large mixing bowl, combine the mixed salad greens, grated carrot, grated beetroot, sliced red cabbage, bell pepper, cherry tomatoes, cucumber, shredded purple cabbage, sliced red onion, and chopped parsley. Add the chopped nuts if using.
3. Make the dressing:
    - In a small bowl, whisk together the olive oil, apple cider vinegar or lemon juice, honey or maple syrup, Dijon mustard, minced garlic, salt, and pepper until well combined.
4. Dress the salad:
    - Pour the dressing over the salad ingredients in the large mixing bowl.
    - Gently toss the salad until all the ingredients are evenly coated with the dressing.
5. Serve:
    - Once dressed, transfer the Rainbow Detox Salad to a serving dish or individual plates.
    - Optionally, garnish with avocado slices, cooked quinoa, cooked chickpeas, or any other additions of your choice.
6. Enjoy:
    - Serve the Rainbow Detox Salad as a nutritious and colorful meal or side dish.
    - Enjoy the variety of flavors and textures in this vibrant salad, packed with vitamins, minerals, and antioxidants!

This Rainbow Detox Salad is not only visually appealing but also nourishing and satisfying. It's a great way to incorporate a wide range of fruits and vegetables into your diet and can be enjoyed as a light meal or side dish. Feel free to customize the ingredients and dressing according to your taste preferences.

Blueberry Spinach Smoothie

Ingredients:

- 1 cup fresh or frozen blueberries
- 1 ripe banana
- 1 cup fresh spinach leaves
- 1/2 cup plain Greek yogurt or dairy-free yogurt
- 1/2 cup almond milk, soy milk, or any milk of your choice
- 1 tablespoon honey or maple syrup (optional, for added sweetness)
- 1/2 teaspoon vanilla extract (optional, for flavor)
- Ice cubes (if using fresh blueberries)

Instructions:

1. Prepare the ingredients:
    - If using fresh blueberries, wash them thoroughly. If using frozen blueberries, there's no need to thaw them.
    - Peel the ripe banana and break it into chunks.
2. Blend the smoothie:
    - In a blender, combine the blueberries, banana chunks, fresh spinach leaves, Greek yogurt or dairy-free yogurt, almond milk or any milk of your choice, honey or maple syrup (if using), and vanilla extract (if using).
    - If you prefer a thicker smoothie, you can add fewer liquid ingredients. If you prefer a thinner consistency, you can add more liquid.
3. Blend until smooth:
    - Blend the ingredients on high speed until smooth and creamy. Stop and scrape down the sides of the blender as needed to ensure all ingredients are well incorporated.
4. Taste and adjust:
    - Taste the smoothie and adjust the sweetness or thickness according to your preference. You can add more honey or maple syrup for added sweetness, or more almond milk for a thinner consistency.
5. Serve:
    - Once blended to your liking, pour the Blueberry Spinach Smoothie into glasses.
    - Optionally, you can add ice cubes to the glasses to make the smoothie colder and more refreshing.

6. Enjoy:
    - Serve the Blueberry Spinach Smoothie immediately and enjoy its refreshing flavor and nutritious goodness!
    - Feel free to garnish with extra blueberries or a sprinkle of chia seeds for added texture and nutrition.

This Blueberry Spinach Smoothie is packed with antioxidants from the blueberries and nutrients from the spinach, making it a healthy and satisfying choice for breakfast or a snack. It's also customizable, so feel free to add your favorite ingredients such as protein powder, flaxseeds, or nut butter to boost its nutritional value even further!

Raw Chocolate Truffles

Ingredients:

- 1 cup pitted dates, soaked in hot water for 10 minutes and drained
- 1 cup raw almonds or cashews
- 3 tablespoons cocoa powder (unsweetened)
- 2 tablespoons coconut oil, melted
- 1 teaspoon vanilla extract
- Pinch of salt
- Optional coatings: shredded coconut, cocoa powder, chopped nuts, or melted dark chocolate for dipping

Instructions:

1. Prepare the ingredients:
    - If the dates are not soft, soak them in hot water for about 10 minutes, then drain well.
    - If you're using whole nuts, you can pulse them in a food processor until finely ground. If you prefer a chunkier texture, you can leave them slightly larger.
2. Blend the truffle mixture:
    - In a food processor, combine the soaked dates, ground almonds or cashews, cocoa powder, melted coconut oil, vanilla extract, and a pinch of salt.
    - Pulse the ingredients until they form a sticky dough-like consistency. Stop and scrape down the sides of the food processor as needed to ensure all ingredients are well incorporated.
3. Form the truffles:
    - Once the mixture is well blended, use your hands to roll it into small balls, about 1 inch in diameter. If the mixture is too sticky, you can wet your hands slightly with water to prevent sticking.
4. Coat the truffles:
    - Roll each truffle ball in your desired coating, such as shredded coconut, cocoa powder, chopped nuts, or leave them plain.
    - Alternatively, you can dip each truffle in melted dark chocolate for a richer coating. Place the coated truffles on a parchment-lined baking sheet.
5. Chill the truffles:

- Once all the truffles are coated, place them in the refrigerator to chill for at least 30 minutes, or until firm.
6. Serve and enjoy:
    - Once chilled, transfer the Raw Chocolate Truffles to an airtight container for storage.
    - Serve and enjoy these decadent treats as a healthy dessert or snack!

These Raw Chocolate Truffles are rich, chocolaty, and satisfying, perfect for satisfying your sweet cravings guilt-free. They're also naturally sweetened with dates and packed with protein and healthy fats from the nuts. Store any leftovers in the refrigerator for up to a week, if they last that long!

Carrot Cake Bites

Ingredients:

- 1 cup shredded carrots (about 2-3 medium carrots)
- 1 cup pitted dates
- 1 cup raw almonds or walnuts
- 1/2 cup shredded coconut (unsweetened)
- 1 teaspoon ground cinnamon
- 1/2 teaspoon ground ginger
- 1/4 teaspoon ground nutmeg
- Pinch of salt
- Optional add-ins: chopped nuts, raisins, dried cranberries, or shredded carrots for extra texture

For the coating (optional):

- Shredded coconut, chopped nuts, cocoa powder, or melted dark chocolate

Instructions:

1. Prepare the ingredients:
    - Wash and peel the carrots, then shred them using a box grater or food processor.
    - Pit the dates if they're not already pitted.
2. Blend the mixture:
    - In a food processor, combine the shredded carrots, pitted dates, raw almonds or walnuts, shredded coconut, ground cinnamon, ground ginger, ground nutmeg, and a pinch of salt.
    - Pulse the ingredients until they form a sticky dough-like consistency. Stop and scrape down the sides of the food processor as needed to ensure all ingredients are well incorporated.
3. Form the carrot cake mixture into bites:
    - Once the mixture is well blended, use your hands to roll it into small balls, about 1 inch in diameter.
    - If the mixture is too sticky, you can wet your hands slightly with water to prevent sticking.
4. Coat the carrot cake bites (optional):

- If desired, roll each carrot cake bite in your desired coating, such as shredded coconut, chopped nuts, cocoa powder, or dip them in melted dark chocolate.
- Place the coated carrot cake bites on a parchment-lined baking sheet.

5. Chill the carrot cake bites:
   - Once all the carrot cake bites are coated, place them in the refrigerator to chill for at least 30 minutes, or until firm.
6. Serve and enjoy:
   - Once chilled, transfer the Carrot Cake Bites to an airtight container for storage.
   - Serve and enjoy these delicious and nutritious snacks as a guilt-free treat!

These Carrot Cake Bites are naturally sweetened with dates and packed with the flavors of carrot cake, including cinnamon, ginger, and nutmeg. They're perfect for snacking on the go, satisfying your sweet cravings, or as a healthy dessert option. Store any leftovers in the refrigerator for up to a week.

Green Goddess Smoothie Bowl

Ingredients:

For the smoothie base:

- 1 ripe banana, frozen
- 1 cup fresh spinach leaves
- 1/2 cup chopped cucumber
- 1/2 cup chopped pineapple (fresh or frozen)
- 1/2 avocado
- 1/2 cup plain Greek yogurt or dairy-free yogurt
- 1 tablespoon chia seeds or ground flaxseeds (optional, for extra fiber)
- 1/2 cup almond milk, coconut water, or any milk of your choice

For topping (customizable):

- Sliced kiwi
- Sliced banana
- Fresh berries (such as strawberries, blueberries, or raspberries)
- Chopped mango
- Granola
- Shredded coconut
- Chia seeds
- Hemp seeds
- Pumpkin seeds
- Nut butter (such as almond butter or peanut butter)
- Drizzle of honey or maple syrup (optional, for added sweetness)

Instructions:

1. Prepare the smoothie base:
    - In a blender, combine the frozen banana, fresh spinach leaves, chopped cucumber, chopped pineapple, avocado, Greek yogurt or dairy-free yogurt, chia seeds or ground flaxseeds (if using), and almond milk or any milk of your choice.

- Blend until smooth and creamy. You may need to stop and scrape down the sides of the blender as needed to ensure all ingredients are well incorporated.
2. Customize the toppings:
    - While the smoothie base is blending, prepare your desired toppings. Wash and slice the fruits as needed. Gather any other toppings you'd like to use, such as granola, shredded coconut, or nut butter.
3. Assemble the smoothie bowl:
    - Pour the smoothie base into a bowl.
    - Arrange your desired toppings over the smoothie base in an aesthetically pleasing manner. Get creative with your toppings and make it look like a work of art!
4. Serve and enjoy:
    - Once assembled, serve the Green Goddess Smoothie Bowl immediately.
    - Enjoy the refreshing and nutritious flavors of this vibrant bowl, packed with vitamins, minerals, and antioxidants!

This Green Goddess Smoothie Bowl is not only delicious but also visually stunning and packed with nutrients from the green fruits, vegetables, and superfoods. It's a perfect way to start your day with a boost of energy and vitality. Feel free to customize the ingredients and toppings according to your taste preferences and dietary needs.

Raw Vegan Cheesecake

Ingredients:

For the crust:

- 1 cup raw almonds or walnuts
- 1 cup pitted dates
- Pinch of salt

For the filling:

- 2 cups raw cashews (soaked in water for at least 4 hours or overnight, then drained)
- 1/2 cup coconut cream (the thick part from a can of full-fat coconut milk)
- 1/4 cup lemon juice
- 1/4 cup maple syrup or agave syrup
- 1/4 cup coconut oil, melted
- 1 teaspoon vanilla extract
- Pinch of salt

For the topping (optional):

- Fresh berries, sliced fruits, or fruit compote

Instructions:

1. Prepare the crust:
    - In a food processor, combine the raw almonds or walnuts, pitted dates, and a pinch of salt.
    - Pulse the ingredients until they form a sticky dough-like consistency. If the mixture is too dry, you can add a few more dates.
2. Press the crust into a pan:
    - Line the bottom of a springform pan with parchment paper.
    - Transfer the crust mixture into the pan and press it evenly onto the bottom to form the crust layer. Use the back of a spoon or your hands to press it down firmly.
3. Prepare the filling:

- In a high-speed blender, combine the soaked and drained cashews, coconut cream, lemon juice, maple syrup or agave syrup, melted coconut oil, vanilla extract, and a pinch of salt.
- Blend the ingredients until smooth and creamy, scraping down the sides of the blender as needed to ensure everything is well combined.

4. Pour the filling over the crust:
    - Once the filling is smooth, pour it over the prepared crust in the springform pan.
    - Use a spatula to smooth out the top to make it even.
5. Chill the cheesecake:
    - Place the cheesecake in the refrigerator to set for at least 4-6 hours, or until firm. For best results, you can also let it chill overnight.
6. Serve and enjoy:
    - Once the cheesecake is set, remove it from the springform pan.
    - Optionally, garnish with fresh berries, sliced fruits, or a fruit compote before serving.
    - Slice and enjoy this delicious Raw Vegan Cheesecake as a guilt-free dessert!

This Raw Vegan Cheesecake is creamy, indulgent, and perfect for those following a vegan or dairy-free lifestyle. It's also naturally sweetened with maple syrup or agave syrup and packed with healthy fats from the nuts and coconut oil. Feel free to get creative with the flavors by adding in cocoa powder for a chocolate version or blending in fruits for different flavor variations.

Tomato Basil Zucchini Pasta

Ingredients:

- 2 medium zucchinis
- 2 tablespoons olive oil
- 3 cloves garlic, minced
- 2 cups cherry tomatoes, halved
- 1/4 cup fresh basil leaves, chopped
- Salt and pepper to taste
- Grated Parmesan cheese or nutritional yeast for serving (optional)

Instructions:

1. Prepare the zucchini noodles:
   - Using a spiralizer or vegetable peeler, spiralize or julienne the zucchinis into long, thin noodles. If using a vegetable peeler, run it along the zucchini lengthwise to create thin strips resembling pasta.
2. Cook the zucchini noodles:
   - Heat 1 tablespoon of olive oil in a large skillet over medium heat.
   - Add the zucchini noodles to the skillet and sauté them for 2-3 minutes, tossing occasionally, until they are just tender but still slightly crisp. Be careful not to overcook them, as they can become mushy.
3. Prepare the tomato basil sauce:
   - In another skillet, heat the remaining 1 tablespoon of olive oil over medium heat.
   - Add the minced garlic to the skillet and sauté for 1-2 minutes until fragrant.
   - Add the halved cherry tomatoes to the skillet and cook for 3-4 minutes, stirring occasionally, until they start to soften and release their juices.
4. Combine the zucchini noodles and sauce:
   - Once the cherry tomatoes are softened, add the cooked zucchini noodles to the skillet with the tomatoes and garlic.
   - Toss everything together gently until the zucchini noodles are evenly coated with the tomato basil sauce.
5. Add the fresh basil and seasonings:
   - Stir in the chopped fresh basil leaves and season the dish with salt and pepper to taste. Adjust the seasoning according to your preference.

6. Serve:
    - Once the zucchini noodles are heated through and the flavors are well combined, remove the skillet from the heat.
    - Optionally, sprinkle grated Parmesan cheese or nutritional yeast over the top for added flavor.
    - Serve the Tomato Basil Zucchini Pasta immediately, either as a light main course or a side dish.

This Tomato Basil Zucchini Pasta is a delicious and nutritious alternative to traditional pasta, and it's ready in just minutes. It's perfect for a quick weeknight dinner or a light and refreshing meal during the summer months. Feel free to customize the recipe by adding additional vegetables, protein, or herbs to suit your taste preferences. Enjoy!

Superfood Salad with Lemon Tahini Dressing

Ingredients:

For the salad:

- 4 cups mixed salad greens (such as spinach, kale, arugula, and/or Swiss chard)
- 1 cup cooked quinoa or any whole grain of your choice (such as farro, bulgur, or brown rice)
- 1 cup mixed superfood vegetables, chopped (such as broccoli florets, shredded carrots, cherry tomatoes, bell peppers, and/or cucumber)
- 1/2 cup cooked chickpeas or beans of your choice (such as black beans or kidney beans)
- 1/4 cup dried fruits (such as cranberries, raisins, or goji berries)
- 1/4 cup nuts or seeds (such as almonds, walnuts, pumpkin seeds, or sunflower seeds)
- Optional add-ins: avocado slices, roasted sweet potato cubes, sliced strawberries, or any other fruits or vegetables you like

For the lemon tahini dressing:

- 1/4 cup tahini (sesame paste)
- 2 tablespoons fresh lemon juice
- 2 tablespoons water
- 1 tablespoon extra virgin olive oil
- 1 clove garlic, minced
- 1 teaspoon honey or maple syrup (optional, for sweetness)
- Salt and pepper to taste

Instructions:

1. Prepare the salad ingredients:
    - Wash and dry the mixed salad greens, then place them in a large mixing bowl.
    - Cook the quinoa or any whole grain according to the package instructions, then let it cool to room temperature.
    - Chop the mixed superfood vegetables into bite-sized pieces.

- Rinse and drain the cooked chickpeas or beans.
- Gather the dried fruits and nuts or seeds.

2. Assemble the salad:
   - Add the cooked quinoa, mixed superfood vegetables, cooked chickpeas or beans, dried fruits, and nuts or seeds to the mixing bowl with the salad greens.
   - Toss everything together gently until well combined. Feel free to add any optional add-ins at this point.

3. Make the lemon tahini dressing:
   - In a small bowl, whisk together the tahini, fresh lemon juice, water, extra virgin olive oil, minced garlic, honey or maple syrup (if using), and a pinch of salt and pepper until smooth and creamy.

4. Dress the salad:
   - Drizzle the lemon tahini dressing over the salad, starting with a small amount and adding more as needed to coat the ingredients evenly.
   - Toss the salad gently to coat it with the dressing.

5. Serve:
   - Once dressed, transfer the Superfood Salad with Lemon Tahini Dressing to serving plates or bowls.
   - Optionally, garnish with additional nuts or seeds, fresh herbs, or a sprinkle of nutritional yeast for extra flavor.

6. Enjoy:
   - Serve the Superfood Salad immediately and enjoy its delicious flavors and nutritious goodness!

This Superfood Salad with Lemon Tahini Dressing is not only tasty but also packed with a variety of nutrients from the mixed greens, quinoa, superfood vegetables, chickpeas, dried fruits, nuts, and seeds. It's a perfect meal for lunch or dinner and can be customized with your favorite ingredients. Enjoy!

www.ingramcontent.com/pod-product-compliance
Lightning Source LLC
LaVergne TN
LVHW062046070526
838201LV00080B/2076